The Complete Sous Vide Cookbook

Mastering the Art of Precision Cooking. 800+ Days of Effortless and Delicious Nutrient-filled Recipes.

Addie C. Lybarger

Table of Contents

Introduction

In recent years, the culinary world has witnessed a profound revolution in the way we approach cooking. Among the myriad of innovative techniques, one stands out for its ability to transform ordinary ingredients into extraordinary gastronomic delights - Sous Vide. This groundbreaking cooking method has captured the hearts of home cooks and professional chefs alike, enabling them to unlock a realm of flavors, textures, and precision previously unattainable in traditional cooking.

Welcome to "The Complete Sous Vide Cookbook," a culinary journey that will elevate your home cooking to new heights of excellence. This comprehensive guide is a celebration of the sous vide technique, offering a rich collection of recipes, techniques, and insights to help you master this artful craft and redefine the way you experience food.

In the pages of this book, you will discover the fascinating history and evolution of sous vide cooking. From its humble beginnings as a method of industrial food preservation to its transition into haute cuisine, you will understand how this culinary phenomenon has grown into a must-have tool in every kitchen.

At the core of sous vide cooking lies the fusion of culinary art and food science. We will delve into the science behind this technique, explaining how precise temperature control, time, and cooking environment work in harmony to create consistent, succulent, and flavorful dishes. This scientific understanding will empower you to experiment with confidence, opening up endless culinary possibilities.

No craft is complete without the proper tools, and sous vide is no exception. From immersion circulators and water baths to vacuum sealers and temperature probes, we will guide you through the essential equipment required to embrace the sous vide method. Moreover, we will detail various sous vide techniques, including pasteurization, infusions, and marinating, to ensure you have a well-rounded understanding of the capabilities of this cooking marvel.

"The Complete Sous Vide Cookbook" presents an exquisite collection of recipes that cater to every palate and occasion. From tender, melt-in-your-mouth steaks and delicate seafood delights to vibrant, perfectly cooked vegetables and luscious desserts, these recipes are designed to showcase the versatility and brilliance of sous vide cooking. Whether you are a seasoned chef or a novice in the kitchen, our step-by-step instructions and tips will help you achieve mouthwatering results.

Sous vide is not only a passport to culinary delights but also a valuable ally in promoting health and wellness. We will explore how sous vide can enhance nutritional value, preserve natural flavors, and reduce the need for added fats and sugars. Embrace a healthier lifestyle without compromising on taste and indulgence.

As you progress on your sous vide journey, we will inspire you to break free from the confines of recipes and explore the world of innovation and creativity. Learn to experiment with different ingredients, flavors, and textures, and create your own signature dishes that reflect your culinary imagination.

In conclusion, "The Complete Sous Vide Cookbook" is a tribute to the transformative power of sous vide cooking. Through this book, you will embark on an adventure that combines science, art, and passion, empowering you to unlock the full potential of your culinary prowess. Whether you are a curious home cook or an aspiring chef, this comprehensive guide will lead you to discover the art of precision cooking and redefine the way you experience food in your own kitchen. Let's embark on this extraordinary culinary journey together. Bon appétit!

Chapter 1. Understanding Sous Vide Cooking

What is Sous Vide?

Sous vide (pronounced "soo veed") is a cooking technique that involves vacuum-sealing food in a bag and cooking it in a precise temperature-controlled water bath. The term "sous vide" is of French origin and translates to "under vacuum," which reflects the vacuum-sealing aspect of the process. This method has gained popularity among both professional chefs and home cooks due to its ability to consistently produce tender, flavorful, and evenly cooked dishes.

The Science behind Sous Vide Cooking

The key principles behind sous vide cooking lie in temperature control and precise cooking times. Traditional cooking methods, like grilling, baking, or frying, often expose food to higher temperatures, leading to a more substantial temperature gradient within the food itself. This can result in overcooking the exterior while undercooking the interior.

In sous vide cooking, the food is placed in an airtight bag, and the air is removed before sealing it. This vacuum-sealing process ensures that the food maintains contact with the water and transfers heat more efficiently. The water bath is then precisely set to the desired temperature, typically lower than traditional cooking methods. This lower temperature allows for more uniform cooking throughout the food, ensuring it reaches the desired doneness without overcooking.

The precise temperature control and longer cooking times in sous vide also facilitate specific chemical reactions in the food. For example, proteins denature at specific temperatures, leading to tenderizing and retaining moisture. Additionally, enzymes and natural flavors in the food are preserved better, resulting in enhanced taste and texture.

Benefits and Advantages of Sous Vide Cooking

a. Consistent Results: One of the most significant advantages of sous vide cooking is its consistency. As the temperature remains constant throughout the cooking process, you can achieve the same level of doneness every time, eliminating the risk of overcooking or undercooking.

b. Retention of Nutrients and Flavors: Sous vide cooking helps preserve the natural flavors, nutrients, and textures of the ingredients. Since the food is sealed in a bag, vitamins and minerals are not lost during cooking, and the flavors are concentrated within the bag.

c. Enhanced Texture and Tenderness: Sous vide cooking allows proteins to break down more gently, resulting in incredibly tender and succulent dishes, particularly meats and fish. Tough cuts of meat can be transformed into melt-in-your-mouth delicacies.

d. Time and Convenience: Although sous vide cooking often requires longer cooking times, it is relatively hands-off. Once the food is in the water bath, there is little risk of overcooking, allowing you to focus on other tasks.

e. Flexibility and Pre-Preparation: Sous vide is excellent for pre-preparing meals. You can cook and vacuum-seal dishes in advance, storing them in the refrigerator or freezer until needed. Reheating the pre-cooked meals requires minimal effort and maintains the original quality.

f. Improved Food Safety: The precise temperature control in sous vide cooking minimizes the risk of foodborne illnesses, as harmful bacteria are killed at specific temperatures.

g. Versatility: Sous vide is not limited to meats; it can be used for vegetables, fruits, eggs, and even desserts. The technique allows for a wide range of culinary experimentation.

Preparing Food for Sous Vide Cooking

Before cooking sous vide, it's essential to properly prepare the food. This includes seasoning, marinating, and vacuum-sealing, if desired. Here are some tips for preparing food for sous vide cooking:

a. Seasoning: Season your food before vacuum-sealing it. This allows the flavors to infuse into the food during the cooking process.

b. Marinating: If you want to add extra flavor to your dish, consider marinating your food before vacuum-sealing it. The extended cooking time of sous vide will allow the flavors to penetrate deeply into the food.

c. Vacuum-Sealing: When using a vacuum sealer, make sure to follow the manufacturer's instructions for sealing the bags correctly. Double-check for any leaks or loose seals that could compromise the cooking process.

Chapter 2. Essential Equipment and Safety Tips

Sous vide is a cooking technique that has gained popularity in recent years for its ability to produce perfectly cooked and tender dishes with minimal effort. The process involves vacuum-sealing food in a bag and cooking it in a water bath at a precise and consistent temperature. This method not only preserves the natural flavors and nutrients of the ingredients but also ensures a higher level of food safety. To achieve the best results and maintain safety during sous vide cooking, certain essential equipment and safety tips are crucial.

Essential Equipment for Sous Vide Cooking

1. Sous Vide Immersion Circulator: The most crucial equipment for sous vide cooking is the immersion circulator. This device attaches to the side of a container filled with water and heats it to a specific temperature, maintaining a constant heat level throughout the cooking process.

2. Vacuum Sealer or Ziplock Bags: To ensure the success of sous vide cooking, a good vacuum sealer or heavy-duty freezer-safe ziplock bags are essential. Properly sealing the food ensures that the flavors are locked in, and there is no risk of water entering the bags.

3. Water Container: You'll need a container that is large enough to hold the food you are cooking and deep enough to accommodate the immersion circulator. Many sous vide enthusiasts use a food-safe plastic or polycarbonate container, but any heat-resistant vessel will work, such as a stainless steel pot or cooler.

4. Heat-Resistant Clips or Weights: To prevent the bags from floating and ensure even cooking, use heat-resistant clips or weights to hold the bags underwater. This is especially important with foods that tend to float, like vegetables.

5. Kitchen Thermometer: Although the immersion circulator maintains a precise temperature, it's always a good idea to have a separate kitchen thermometer to verify the water temperature periodically.

6. Lid or Plastic Wrap: Using a lid or plastic wrap to cover the water container helps retain heat and prevents water evaporation during long cooking times.

7. Tongs and Slotted Spoon: Handling hot food packages can be tricky. Tongs and a slotted spoon are useful for removing bags from the water bath without risk of burning yourself.

Safety Tips for Sous Vide Cooking

1. Food Safety: One of the significant benefits of sous vide cooking is that it ensures food safety by cooking at precise temperatures. However, it is crucial to use fresh, high-quality ingredients and follow standard food safety guidelines. Always ensure that the food is properly cleaned, and if marinating, do so in the refrigerator, not at room temperature.

2. Water Safety: The water used in the sous vide process should be potable and safe for consumption. If you are using tap water, be aware of any potential contaminants. For added safety, consider using filtered water or bottled water.

3. Proper Vacuum Sealing: When using a vacuum sealer, it's essential to seal the bags correctly. Double-check for any leaks or incomplete seals before immersing them in the water bath. If using ziplock bags, try the water displacement method to remove air before sealing.

4. Preventing Bag Leaks: To minimize the risk of bag leaks, avoid overfilling the bags. Leave enough room for the food to expand slightly during cooking, but don't leave too much space, as this can cause uneven cooking.

5. Avoid Cross-Contamination: When preparing multiple bags of food, be cautious not to cross-contaminate different ingredients. Use separate cutting boards, utensils, and preparation areas for raw meats, vegetables, and other foods.

6. Temperature Control: Ensure the accuracy of your sous vide device by calibrating it with a reliable kitchen thermometer. Periodically check the water temperature during long cooking sessions to make sure it remains consistent.

7. Cooking Time and Temperatures: Follow recipes and cooking guidelines closely. Different foods require specific temperatures and cooking times for safe and optimal results. Using sous vide charts and guides can be helpful.

8. Chill and Store Safely: After sous vide cooking, quickly chill the food in an ice bath or cold water before storing it in the refrigerator or freezer. This prevents bacterial growth and preserves the quality of the food.

9. Reheating Sous Vide Food: If you plan to reheat sous vide food, do so quickly and efficiently. While sous vide cooking is safe for long-duration cooking, reheating requires caution to avoid the risk of foodborne illnesses.

10. Don't Leave Unattended: Although sous vide cooking is a relatively hands-off method, it is essential not to leave the equipment unattended during the cooking process. Keep a close eye on the water level and the overall cooking progress.

Time and Temperature Guidelines

One of the great advantages of sous vide cooking is the precision it offers in terms of cooking time and temperature. Different foods require different cooking times and temperatures, so it's crucial to follow guidelines to achieve optimal results. Sous vide recipes often provide recommended time and temperature settings for various dishes, but here are some general guidelines:

a. Proteins:

Beef: Medium-rare (130°F / 54°C) to well-done (160°F / 71°C)
Chicken: 140°F / 60°C to 165°F / 74°C
Fish: 120°F / 49°C to 145°F / 63°C (varies depending on the fish)
b. Vegetables:

Tender Vegetables (asparagus, green beans): 183°F / 84°C
Firm Vegetables (carrots, beets): 185°F / 85°C

The Sous Vide Cooking Process

Now that you have your equipment ready and your food prepared, it's time to start cooking! The sous vide cooking process typically involves the following steps:

a. Preheat the Water Bath: Set up your water bath and preheat it to the desired temperature using your immersion circulator.

b. Place the Food in the Water Bath: Carefully lower the vacuum-sealed bags into the water bath, ensuring that they are fully submerged. Use sous vide weights or clips to keep the bags from floating.

c. Cook for the Required Time: Cook the food for the recommended time based on the cooking temperature and the type of food you're preparing.

d. Finishing Step: After the cooking time is complete, remove the food from the water bath. If you are cooking meat, you can sear it briefly in a hot pan or use a culinary torch to add color and texture to the exterior.

Chapter 3. Breakfast

1. Egg Bites

Preparation Time: 15 minutes

Cooking Time: 60 minutes

Servings: 4

Ingredients:

- 6 large eggs
- 1/2 cup shredded cheddar cheese
- 1/4 cup cottage cheese
- 1/4 cup chopped cooked bacon
- 1/4 cup chopped spinach
- Salt and pepper to taste

Directions:

1. Preheat the sous vide water bath to 167°F (75°C).
2. In a blender, combine eggs, cheddar cheese, cottage cheese, bacon, and spinach. Season with salt and pepper.
3. Pour the mixture into 4-ounce mason jars and close the lids loosely.
4. Submerge the jars in the water bath and cook for 60 minutes.
5. Remove the jars from the water bath, let them cool for a few minutes, and then serve.

Nutrition: Calories: 230kcal; Fat: 15g; Carb: 4g; Protein: 18g

2. Oatmeal

Preparation Time: 5 minutes

Cooking Time: 1 hour

Servings: 2

Ingredients:

- 1 cup rolled oats
- 2 cups milk (dairy or plant-based)
- 2 tablespoons maple syrup
- 1/2 teaspoon ground cinnamon
- Pinch of salt
- Fresh berries for topping

Directions:

1. Preheat the sous vide water bath to 154°F (68°C).
2. In a vacuum-sealed bag, combine oats, milk, maple syrup, cinnamon, and salt.
3. Seal the bag and submerge it in the water bath.
4. Cook for 1 hour.
5. Open the bag, give it a stir, and serve with fresh berries on top.

Nutrition: Calories: 300kcal; Fat: 6g; Carb: 50g; Protein: 12g

3. Breakfast Burritos

Preparation Time: 20 minutes

Cooking Time: 2 hours

Servings: 4

Ingredients:

- 4 large eggs
- 1/2 cup diced bell peppers
- 1/2 cup diced onions
- 1/2 cup diced tomatoes
- 1/4 cup shredded cheddar cheese
- 4 large flour tortillas
- Salt and pepper to taste
- Salsa and avocado for serving

Directions:

1. Preheat the sous vide water bath to 167°F (75°C).
2. In a bowl, whisk the eggs and season with salt and pepper.
3. Divide the diced bell peppers, onions, tomatoes, and shredded cheddar cheese among the tortillas.
4. Pour the whisked eggs over the fillings in each tortilla.
5. Roll up the tortillas tightly, ensuring the fillings are enclosed.
6. Place the burritos in vacuum-sealed bags and seal them.
7. Submerge the bags in the water bath and cook for 2 hours.
8. Remove the burritos from the bags, slice them in half, and serve with salsa and avocado.

Nutrition: Calories: 380kcal; Fat: 18g; Carb: 37g; Protein: 16g

4. Banana Pancakes

Preparation Time: 10 minutes

Cooking Time: 1 hour

Servings: 2

Ingredients:

- 1 ripe banana, mashed

- 2 large eggs
- 1/2 cup almond flour
- 1/2 teaspoon baking powder
- 1/4 teaspoon ground cinnamon
- Maple syrup and fresh bananas for serving

Directions:

1. Preheat the sous vide water bath to 155°F (68°C).
2. In a bowl, mix the mashed banana, eggs, almond flour, baking powder, and cinnamon until well combined.
3. Let the batter rest for a few minutes.
4. Pour the batter into a vacuum-sealed bag and seal it.
5. Submerge the bag in the water bath and cook for 1 hour.
6. Carefully remove the bag from the water bath, cut it open, and slide the pancake onto a plate.
7. Drizzle with maple syrup and serve with fresh banana slices.

Nutrition: Calories: 350kcal; Fat: 21g; Carb: 31g; Protein: 13g

5. Breakfast Casserole

Preparation Time: 20 minutes

Cooking Time: 2 hours

Servings: 6

Ingredients:

- 6 large eggs
- 1 cup milk (dairy or plant-based)
- 1 cup diced ham
- 1 cup diced bell peppers
- 1 cup diced onions
- 1 cup shredded cheddar cheese
- 1 teaspoon dried thyme
- Salt and pepper to taste

Directions:

1. Preheat the sous vide water bath to 167°F (75°C).
2. In a bowl, whisk the eggs, milk, dried thyme, salt, and pepper.
3. In a separate bowl, mix the diced ham, bell peppers, onions, and shredded cheddar cheese.
4. Grease a casserole dish and layer the ham mixture evenly.
5. Pour the egg mixture over the ham mixture.
6. Cover the casserole dish tightly with foil.
7. Submerge the dish in the water bath and cook for 2 hours.

8. Remove the casserole from the water bath, let it cool slightly, and then cut into slices to serve.

Nutrition: Calories: 320kcal; Fat: 21g; Carb: 8g; Protein: 23g

6. Avocado and Bacon Toast

Preparation Time: 10 minutes

Cooking Time: 1 hour

Servings: 2

Ingredients:

- 2 slices whole-grain bread
- 1 ripe avocado, mashed
- 4 slices cooked bacon
- 2 poached eggs
- Salt and pepper to taste
- Red pepper flakes (optional)

Directions:

1. Preheat the sous vide water bath to 145°F (63°C).
2. Spread the mashed avocado on each slice of bread.
3. Top each slice with 2 slices of cooked bacon.
4. Gently lower the poached eggs into separate vacuum-sealed bags.
5. Submerge the bags in the water bath and cook for 1 hour.
6. Remove the poached eggs from the bags and place them on top of the bacon.
7. Season with salt, pepper, and red pepper flakes if desired.

Nutrition: Calories: 380kcal; Fat: 24g; Carb: 26g; Protein: 15g

7. French Toast

Preparation Time: 15 minutes

Cooking Time: 2 hours

Servings: 4

Ingredients:

- 4 thick slices of brioche or challah bread
- 4 large eggs
- 1 cup milk (dairy or plant-based)
- 1 teaspoon vanilla extract
- 1/2 teaspoon ground cinnamon
- Butter or oil for cooking
- Maple syrup and fresh berries for serving

Directions:

1. Preheat the sous vide water bath to 154°F (68°C).
2. In a shallow dish, whisk together eggs, milk, vanilla extract, and ground cinnamon.
3. Dip each slice of bread into the egg mixture, coating both sides.
4. Place the coated slices of bread in vacuum-sealed bags, ensuring they lie flat.
5. Seal the bags and submerge them in the water bath.
6. Cook for 2 hours.
7. Remove the bags from the water bath, carefully open them, and transfer the French toast to a plate.
8. Heat a skillet over medium heat with butter or oil.
9. Sear each side of the French toast until golden brown.
10. Serve with maple syrup and fresh berries.

Nutrition: Calories: 390kcal; Fat: 17g; Carb: 45g; Protein: 15g

8. Shakshuka

Preparation Time: 15 minutes

Cooking Time: 1 hour

Servings: 4

Ingredients:

- 1 tablespoon olive oil
- 1 large onion, diced
- 1 red bell pepper, diced
- 2 cloves garlic, minced
- 1 can (14 oz) diced tomatoes
- 1 teaspoon ground cumin
- 1 teaspoon ground paprika
- 1/2 teaspoon ground cayenne pepper (optional)
- Salt and pepper to taste
- 4-6 large eggs
- Fresh parsley for garnish

Directions:

1. Preheat the sous vide water bath to 176°F (80°C).
2. In a skillet, heat the olive oil over medium heat.
3. Add the diced onion and red bell pepper, and sauté until softened.
4. Stir in the minced garlic, diced tomatoes, ground cumin, ground paprika, cayenne pepper (if using), salt, and pepper. Let the mixture simmer for a few minutes.
5. Transfer the mixture to a vacuum-sealed bag and seal it.
6. Submerge the bag in the water bath and cook for 1 hour.
7. Remove the bag from the water bath, open it carefully, and transfer the shakshuka to a serving dish.

8. Create wells in the shakshuka and crack the eggs into the wells.

9. Return the dish to the water bath and cook for an additional 10-15 minutes until the eggs are cooked to your desired level.

10. Garnish with fresh parsley before serving.

Nutrition: Calories: 180kcal; Fat: 11g; Carb: 12g; Protein: 10g

9. Frittata

Preparation Time: 15 minutes

Cooking Time: 1 hour

Servings: 4

Ingredients:

- 8 large eggs
- 1/2 cup milk (dairy or plant-based)
- 1 cup diced cooked ham
- 1 cup diced bell peppers
- 1 cup chopped spinach
- 1/2 cup shredded cheddar cheese
- Salt and pepper to taste

Directions:

1. Preheat the sous vide water bath to 167°F (75°C).

2. In a bowl, whisk together eggs, milk, salt, and pepper.

3. Stir in the diced ham, bell peppers, spinach, and shredded cheddar cheese.

4. Pour the mixture into a greased baking dish.

5. Cover the dish with foil.

6. Submerge the dish in the water bath and cook for 1 hour.

7. Carefully remove the dish from the water bath, let it cool slightly, and then slice into wedges to serve.

Nutrition: Calories: 280kcal; Fat: 18g; Carb: 6g; Protein: 22g

10. Blueberry Pancakes

Preparation Time: 10 minutes

Cooking Time: 1 hour

Servings: 2

Ingredients:

- 1 cup all-purpose flour
- 1 tablespoon sugar
- 1 teaspoon baking powder
- 1/2 teaspoon baking soda

- 1/2 teaspoon salt
- 3/4 cup buttermilk
- 1 large egg
- 1 tablespoon melted butter
- 1/2 cup fresh blueberries
- Maple syrup and extra blueberries for serving

Directions:

1. Preheat the sous vide water bath to 145°F (63°C).
2. In a large bowl, whisk together flour, sugar, baking powder, baking soda, and salt.
3. In a separate bowl, whisk together buttermilk, egg, and melted butter.
4. Combine the wet and dry ingredients, then gently fold in the fresh blueberries.
5. Pour the pancake batter into a vacuum-sealed bag and seal it.
6. Submerge the bag in the water bath and cook for 1 hour.
7. Remove the bag from the water bath, open it carefully, and slide the pancakes onto a plate.
8. Serve with maple syrup and additional fresh blueberries.

Nutrition: Calories: 320kcal; Fat: 8g; Carb: 53g; Protein: 10g

11. Chia Seed Pudding

Preparation Time: 5 minutes

Cooking Time: 2 hours

Servings: 4

Ingredients:

- 1 cup coconut milk (canned)
- 1/4 cup chia seeds
- 2 tablespoons honey or maple syrup
- 1 teaspoon vanilla extract
- Fresh fruit and shredded coconut for topping

Directions:

1. Preheat the sous vide water bath to 140°F (60°C).
2. In a bowl, mix together coconut milk, chia seeds, honey or maple syrup, and vanilla extract.
3. Divide the mixture among four small mason jars.
4. Close the lids loosely and submerge the jars in the water bath.
5. Cook for 2 hours.
6. Remove the jars from the water bath, tighten the lids, and refrigerate for at least 4 hours or overnight.
7. Top with fresh fruit and shredded coconut before serving.

Nutrition: Calories: 180kcal; Fat: 13g; Carb: 15g; Protein: 4g

12. Veggie Hash

Preparation Time: 15 minutes

Cooking Time: 1 hour

Servings: 4

Ingredients:

- 2 cups diced sweet potatoes
- 1 cup diced bell peppers
- 1 cup diced zucchini
- 1 cup diced red onion
- 2 tablespoons olive oil
- 1 teaspoon paprika
- 1/2 teaspoon garlic powder
- Salt and pepper to taste
- 4 poached eggs
- Fresh cilantro for garnish

Directions:

1. Preheat the sous vide water bath to 185°F (85°C).
2. In a bowl, toss together diced sweet potatoes, bell peppers, zucchini, and red onion with olive oil, paprika, garlic powder, salt, and pepper.
3. Place the seasoned vegetables in a vacuum-sealed bag and seal it.
4. Submerge the bag in the water bath and cook for 1 hour.
5. Remove the bag from the water bath, open it carefully, and transfer the hash to a serving dish.
6. Top each portion with a poached egg and garnish with fresh cilantro.

Nutrition: Calories: 220kcal; Fat: 10g; Carb: 26g; Protein: 8g

13. Cinnamon Apple Porridge

Preparation Time: 10 minutes

Cooking Time: 2 hours

Servings: 2

Ingredients:

- 1 cup steel-cut oats
- 2 cups water
- 1 cup milk (dairy or plant-based)
- 1 apple, diced
- 1 tablespoon honey
- 1 teaspoon ground cinnamon

- 1/4 teaspoon ground nutmeg
- Pinch of salt
- Chopped nuts and a drizzle of honey for serving

Directions:

1. Preheat the sous vide water bath to 154°F (68°C).
2. In a bowl, combine steel-cut oats, water, milk, diced apple, honey, ground cinnamon, ground nutmeg, and a pinch of salt.
3. Pour the mixture into a vacuum-sealed bag and seal it.
4. Submerge the bag in the water bath and cook for 2 hours.
5. Remove the bag from the water bath, open it carefully, and transfer the porridge to bowls.
6. Top with chopped nuts and a drizzle of honey before serving.

Nutrition: Calories: 360kcal; Fat: 8g; Carb: 64g; Protein: 10g

14. Breakfast Sausage Patties

Preparation Time: 15 minutes

Cooking Time: 2 hours

Servings: 6

Ingredients:

- 1 pound ground pork
- 1 teaspoon dried sage
- 1/2 teaspoon dried thyme
- 1/2 teaspoon garlic powder
- 1/2 teaspoon onion powder
- 1/4 teaspoon ground black pepper
- 1/4 teaspoon salt
- Pinch of red pepper flakes (optional)

Directions:

1. Preheat the sous vide water bath to 140°F (60°C).
2. In a bowl, mix together ground pork, dried sage, dried thyme, garlic powder, onion powder, black pepper, salt, and red pepper flakes (if using).
3. Form the mixture into 6 patties and place them on a plate.
4. Transfer the plate to the freezer for about 15 minutes to firm up the patties.
5. Once the patties are firm, place them in a vacuum-sealed bag and seal it.
6. Submerge the bag in the water bath and cook for 2 hours.
7. Remove the bag from the water bath, open it carefully, and transfer the sausage patties to a skillet.
8. Sear the patties over medium-high heat until they are browned on both sides.

Nutrition: Calories: 190kcal; Fat: 14g; Carb: 1g; Protein: 14g

15. Breakfast Tacos

Preparation Time: 15 minutes

Cooking Time: 1 hour

Servings: 4

Ingredients:

- 8 small corn or flour tortillas
- 4 large eggs
- 1 cup black beans, cooked and drained
- 1 cup diced tomatoes
- 1 cup diced avocado
- 1/4 cup chopped cilantro
- 1/4 cup crumbled queso fresco or feta cheese
- Lime wedges for serving
- Hot sauce (optional)

Directions:

1. Preheat the sous vide water bath to 167°F (75°C).
2. Warm the tortillas by wrapping them in foil and placing them in the water bath for a few minutes.
3. In a bowl, whisk the eggs and season with salt and pepper.
4. Pour the whisked eggs into a vacuum-sealed bag and seal it.
5. Submerge the bag in the water bath and cook for 1 hour.
6. Remove the bag from the water bath, open it carefully, and transfer the scrambled eggs to a serving dish.
7. Assemble the tacos by placing scrambled eggs, black beans, diced tomatoes, diced avocado, chopped cilantro, and crumbled queso fresco or feta cheese in each tortilla.
8. Serve with lime wedges and hot sauce on the side.

Nutrition: Calories: 300kcal; Fat: 12g; Carb: 38g; Protein: 12g

Chapter 4.   Starters and Small Bites

16. Garlic Butter Shrimp

Preparation Time: 10 minutes

Cooking Time: 30 minutes

Servings: 4

Ingredients:

- 1 lb (450g) large shrimp, peeled and deveined
- 4 tbsp unsalted butter, melted
- 4 cloves garlic, minced
- 1 tsp lemon zest
- Salt and pepper to taste

Directions:

1. Preheat the sous vide water bath to 135°F (57°C).
2. In a bowl, mix melted butter, minced garlic, lemon zest, salt, and pepper.
3. Divide the shrimp into vacuum-sealed bags and pour the garlic butter mixture over them.
4. Seal the bags using a vacuum sealer and cook in the water bath for 30 minutes.
5. Remove the shrimp from the bags and serve hot. You can also sear them briefly in a hot pan before serving.

Nutrition: Calories: 210kcal; Fat: 12g; Carb: 1g; Protein: 22g

17. Beef Sliders

Preparation Time: 15 minutes

Cooking Time: 2 hours

Servings: 6

Ingredients:

- 1 lb (450g) ground beef
- 1/2 onion, finely chopped
- 1 garlic clove, minced
- 1 tbsp Worcestershire sauce
- Salt and pepper to taste
- Slider buns, lettuce, and tomato slices for serving

Directions:

1. Preheat the sous vide water bath to 135°F (57°C).

2. In a bowl, mix ground beef, chopped onion, minced garlic, Worcestershire sauce, salt, and pepper.

3. Form small patties and place each patty in a separate vacuum-sealed bag.

4. Cook the patties in the water bath for 2 hours.

5. Remove the patties from the bags and sear them on a hot grill or pan for 1 minute per side.

6. Assemble the sliders with lettuce, tomato slices, and your favorite condiments.

Nutrition: Calories: 280kcal; Fat: 18g; Carb: 6g; Protein: 22g

18. Artichoke Hearts with Lemon Herb Dip

Preparation Time: 10 minutes

Cooking Time: 1 hour

Servings: 4

Ingredients:

- 1 can (14 oz) artichoke hearts, drained
- 2 tbsp olive oil
- 1 tsp dried thyme
- 1 tsp dried oregano
- Zest of 1 lemon
- Salt and pepper to taste

Directions:

1. Preheat the sous vide water bath to 185°F (85°C).

2. Toss the artichoke hearts with olive oil, dried thyme, dried oregano, lemon zest, salt, and pepper.

3. Place the seasoned artichoke hearts in a vacuum-sealed bag.

4. Cook the artichoke hearts in the water bath for 1 hour.

5. Serve the artichoke hearts warm with a lemon herb dip made by mixing Greek yogurt, lemon juice, chopped fresh herbs, salt, and pepper.

Nutrition: Calories: 150kcal; Fat: 10g; Carb: 12g; Protein: 3g

19. Buffalo Cauliflower Bites

Preparation Time: 15 minutes

Cooking Time: 1 hour

Servings: 4

Ingredients:

- 1 head cauliflower, cut into bite-sized florets
- 1/4 cup hot sauce
- 2 tbsp unsalted butter, melted
- 1 tsp garlic powder
- Salt and pepper to taste

Directions:

1. Preheat the sous vide water bath to 185°F (85°C).
2. In a bowl, mix hot sauce, melted butter, garlic powder, salt, and pepper.
3. Toss the cauliflower florets with the hot sauce mixture until evenly coated.
4. Place the cauliflower in a vacuum-sealed bag.
5. Cook the cauliflower in the water bath for 1 hour.
6. After cooking, transfer the cauliflower to a baking sheet and broil in the oven for 5 minutes to crisp up the edges.
7. Serve the buffalo cauliflower bites with ranch dressing or blue cheese dip.

Nutrition: Calories: 120kcal; Fat: 7g; Carb: 12g; Protein: 4g

20. Stuffed Mushrooms

Preparation Time: 20 minutes

Cooking Time: 1 hour

Servings: 6

Ingredients:

- 12 large button mushrooms, stems removed and reserved
- 1/2 cup cream cheese
- 1/4 cup grated Parmesan cheese
- 2 tbsp chopped fresh parsley
- 1 garlic clove, minced
- Salt and pepper to taste

Directions:

1. Preheat the sous vide water bath to 185°F (85°C).
2. In a bowl, mix cream cheese, grated Parmesan, chopped parsley, minced garlic, salt, and pepper.
3. Fill each mushroom cap with the cream cheese mixture.
4. Place the stuffed mushrooms in a vacuum-sealed bag.
5. Cook the mushrooms in the water bath for 1 hour.
6. Remove the mushrooms from the bags and serve hot.

Nutrition: Calories: 90kcal; Fat: 7g; Carb: 2g; Protein: 5g

21. Asparagus Wrapped in Prosciutto

Preparation Time: 10 minutes

Cooking Time: 30 minutes

Servings: 4

Ingredients:

- 1 bunch asparagus, tough ends trimmed
- 8 slices prosciutto
- 2 tbsp olive oil
- 1 tsp lemon juice
- 1/2 tsp lemon zest
- Salt and pepper to taste

Directions:

1. Preheat the sous vide water bath to 185°F (85°C).
2. Toss the asparagus with olive oil, lemon juice, lemon zest, salt, and pepper.
3. Wrap two asparagus spears with a slice of prosciutto.
4. Place the wrapped asparagus bundles in a vacuum-sealed bag.
5. Cook the asparagus in the water bath for 30 minutes.
6. Remove the asparagus from the bags and serve warm.

Nutrition: Calories: 150kcal; Fat: 10g; Carb: 5g; Protein: 10g

22. Deviled Eggs

Preparation Time: 15 minutes

Cooking Time: 1 hour

Servings: 8

Ingredients:

- 8 large eggs
- 1/4 cup mayonnaise
- 1 tsp Dijon mustard
- 1 tsp white wine vinegar
- 1/4 tsp paprika
- Salt and pepper to taste
- Chopped chives for garnish

Directions:

1. Preheat the sous vide water bath to 167°F (75°C).
2. Gently place the eggs in the water bath and cook for 1 hour.
3. Once cooked, remove the eggs from the water bath and let them cool.
4. Peel the eggs and cut them in half. Remove the yolks and place them in a bowl.
5. Mash the egg yolks with mayonnaise, Dijon mustard, white wine vinegar, paprika, salt, and pepper until smooth.
6. Fill the egg white halves with the yolk mixture.
7. Garnish with chopped chives and serve.

Nutrition: Calories: 140kcal; Fat: 12g; Carb: 1g; Protein: 6g

23. Sweet Potato Bites

Preparation Time: 10 minutes

Cooking Time: 1 hour

Servings: 4

Ingredients:

- 2 large sweet potatoes, peeled and cut into bite-sized cubes
- 2 tbsp olive oil
- 1 tsp smoked paprika
- 1/2 tsp ground cumin
- Salt and pepper to taste

Directions:

1. Preheat the sous vide water bath to 185°F (85°C).
2. Toss the sweet potato cubes with olive oil, smoked paprika, ground cumin, salt, and pepper.
3. Place the seasoned sweet potatoes in a vacuum-sealed bag.
4. Cook the sweet potatoes in the water bath for 1 hour.
5. Remove the sweet potatoes from the bags and serve warm.

Nutrition: Calories: 180kcal; Fat: 8g; Carb: 28g; Protein: 2g

24. Chicken Skewers with Peanut Sauce

Preparation Time: 20 minutes

Cooking Time: 1 hour

Servings: 4

Ingredients:

- 1 lb (450g) boneless, skinless chicken breasts, cut into cubes
- 1/4 cup soy sauce
- 2 tbsp honey
- 1 tsp sesame oil
- 1/2 tsp ground ginger
- 1/4 cup peanut butter
- 2 tbsp water
- Chopped peanuts and sliced green onions for garnish

Directions:

1. Preheat the sous vide water bath to 145°F (63°C).
2. In a bowl, mix soy sauce, honey, sesame oil, and ground ginger.
3. Thread the chicken cubes onto skewers and place them in a vacuum-sealed bag.
4. Pour the marinade over the chicken skewers.

5. Cook the chicken skewers in the water bath for 1 hour.

6. In a separate bowl, whisk peanut butter and water to make the sauce.

7. Serve the sous vide chicken skewers with peanut sauce and garnish with chopped peanuts and sliced green onions.

Nutrition: Calories: 320kcal; Fat: 16g; Carb: 15g; Protein: 30g

25. Beet and Goat Cheese Salad

Preparation Time: 15 minutes

Cooking Time: 2 hours

Servings: 4

Ingredients:

- 2 large beets, peeled and sliced
- 1 tbsp olive oil
- 2 tbsp balsamic vinegar
- 1/4 cup crumbled goat cheese
- 1/4 cup chopped walnuts
- Salt and pepper to taste

Directions:

Preheat the sous vide water bath to 185°F (85°C).

Toss the sliced beets with olive oil, balsamic vinegar, salt, and pepper.

Place the seasoned beets in a vacuum-sealed bag.

Cook the beets in the water bath for 2 hours.

Remove the beets from the bags and let them cool slightly.

Arrange the beet slices on a plate, sprinkle with crumbled goat cheese and chopped walnuts.

Drizzle with extra balsamic vinegar if desired and serve.

Nutrition: Calories: 180kcal; Fat: 12g; Carb: 15g; Protein: 5g

26. Caprese Skewers

Preparation Time: 10 minutes

Cooking Time: 1 hour

Servings: 4

Ingredients:

- 1 pint cherry tomatoes
- 8 oz fresh mozzarella balls
- Fresh basil leaves
- Balsamic glaze
- Salt and pepper to taste

Directions:

1. Preheat the sous vide water bath to 125°F (52°C).
2. Thread cherry tomatoes, fresh mozzarella balls, and basil leaves onto skewers.
3. Season the skewers with salt and pepper.
4. Place the skewers in a vacuum-sealed bag.
5. Cook the skewers in the water bath for 1 hour.
6. Remove the skewers from the bags and arrange them on a serving platter.
7. Drizzle with balsamic glaze before serving.

Nutrition: Calories: 140kcal; Fat: 9g; Carb: 5g; Protein: 10g

27. Lemon Herb Salmon Bites

Preparation Time: 10 minutes

Cooking Time: 40 minutes

Servings: 4

Ingredients:

- 1 lb (450g) salmon fillets, cut into bite-sized pieces
- 2 tbsp olive oil
- Juice and zest of 1 lemon
- 2 cloves garlic, minced
- 1 tbsp chopped fresh dill
- Salt and pepper to taste

Directions:

1. Preheat the sous vide water bath to 130°F (54°C).
2. In a bowl, mix olive oil, lemon juice, lemon zest, minced garlic, chopped dill, salt, and pepper.
3. Place the salmon pieces in a vacuum-sealed bag.
4. Pour the lemon herb mixture over the salmon.
5. Cook the salmon in the water bath for 40 minutes.
6. Remove the salmon from the bags and serve warm.

Nutrition: Calories: 230kcal; Fat: 14g; Carb: 2g; Protein: 25g

28. Gorgonzola-Stuffed Dates

Preparation Time: 10 minutes

Cooking Time: 1 hour

Servings: 4

Ingredients:

- 12 Medjool dates, pitted
- 2 oz Gorgonzola cheese

- 1/4 cup chopped walnuts
- Honey for drizzling

Directions:

1. Preheat the sous vide water bath to 135°F (57°C).
2. Stuff each date with a small piece of Gorgonzola cheese and a pinch of chopped walnuts.
3. Place the stuffed dates in a vacuum-sealed bag.
4. Cook the dates in the water bath for 1 hour.
5. Remove the dates from the bags and arrange them on a serving platter.
6. Drizzle with honey before serving.

Nutrition: Calories: 170kcal; Fat: 6g; Carb: 28g; Protein: 3g

29. Lemon-Garlic Artichoke Hearts

Preparation Time: 10 minutes

Cooking Time: 1 hour

Servings: 4

Ingredients:

- 1 can (14 oz) artichoke hearts, drained and halved
- 2 tbsp olive oil
- Juice and zest of 1 lemon
- 2 cloves garlic, minced
- Salt and pepper to taste

Directions:

1. Preheat the sous vide water bath to 185°F (85°C).
2. Toss the halved artichoke hearts with olive oil, lemon juice, lemon zest, minced garlic, salt, and pepper.
3. Place the seasoned artichoke hearts in a vacuum-sealed bag.
4. Cook the artichoke hearts in the water bath for 1 hour.
5. Remove the artichoke hearts from the bags and serve warm.

Nutrition: Calories: 120kcal; Fat: 8g; Carb: 10g; Protein: 2g

30. Rosemary Balsamic Steak Bites

Preparation Time: 15 minutes

Cooking Time: 2 hours

Servings: 4

Ingredients:

- 1 lb (450g) sirloin steak, cut into bite-sized pieces
- 1/4 cup balsamic vinegar
- 2 tbsp olive oil

- 2 sprigs fresh rosemary
- Salt and pepper to taste

Directions:

1. Preheat the sous vide water bath to 135°F (57°C).
2. In a bowl, mix balsamic vinegar, olive oil, fresh rosemary, salt, and pepper.
3. Place the steak pieces in a vacuum-sealed bag.
4. Pour the balsamic mixture over the steak.
5. Cook the steak bites in the water bath for 2 hours.
6. Remove the steak bites from the bags and sear them on a hot grill or pan for 1 minute per side.
7. Serve the sous vide steak bites warm.

Nutrition: Calories: 280kcal; Fat: 16g; Carb: 2g; Protein: 30g

Chapter 5. Seafood

31. Garlic Butter Shrimp

Preparation Time: 15 minutes

Cooking Time: 30 minutes

Servings: 4

Ingredients:

- 1 lb (450g) large shrimp, peeled and deveined
- 4 tbsp butter, melted
- 4 cloves garlic, minced
- 1 tsp dried parsley
- 1/2 tsp salt
- 1/4 tsp black pepper
- 1/4 tsp red pepper flakes (optional)

Directions:

1. Preheat the sous vide water bath to 135°F (57°C).
2. In a bowl, mix melted butter, minced garlic, dried parsley, salt, black pepper, and red pepper flakes.
3. Place the cleaned shrimp in a vacuum-sealed bag and pour the garlic butter mixture over it.
4. Seal the bag and cook in the sous vide water bath for 30 minutes.
5. Once done, remove the shrimp from the bag and serve immediately.

Nutrition: Calories: 230kcal; Fat: 14g; Carb: 2g; Protein: 24g

32. Lemon Dill Salmon

Preparation Time: 10 minutes

Cooking Time: 1 hour

Servings: 2

Ingredients:

- 2 salmon fillets
- 1 lemon, thinly sliced
- 2 sprigs fresh dill
- 1 tbsp olive oil
- Salt and pepper to taste

Directions:

1. Preheat the sous vide water bath to 125°F (52°C) for medium-rare doneness or 135°F (57°C) for medium doneness.
2. Season the salmon fillets with salt and pepper and place them in separate vacuum-sealed bags.
3. Add lemon slices, fresh dill, and a drizzle of olive oil to each bag.
4. Seal the bags and cook in the sous vide water bath for 1 hour.
5. Remove the salmon from the bags and serve with additional fresh dill and lemon slices if desired.

Nutrition: Calories: 350kcal; Fat: 22g; Carb: 4g; Protein: 34g

33. Lobster Tails with Garlic Butter

Preparation Time: 20 minutes

Cooking Time: 40 minutes

Servings: 2

Ingredients:

- 2 lobster tails
- 4 tbsp butter, melted
- 2 cloves garlic, minced
- 1 tbsp fresh parsley, chopped
- 1/2 tsp salt
- 1/4 tsp black pepper

Directions:

1. Preheat the sous vide water bath to 140°F (60°C).
2. Butterfly the lobster tails by cutting the top shell lengthwise and carefully pulling the meat upward.
3. In a bowl, mix melted butter, minced garlic, chopped parsley, salt, and black pepper.
4. Place each lobster tail in a separate vacuum-sealed bag and pour the garlic butter mixture over them.
5. Seal the bags and cook in the sous vide water bath for 40 minutes.
6. Once done, remove the lobster tails from the bags and serve with additional melted butter on the side.

Nutrition: Calories: 280kcal; Fat: 18g; Carb: 2g; Protein: 28g

34. Scallop Risotto

Preparation Time: 15 minutes

Cooking Time: 1 hour

Servings: 4

Ingredients:

- 1 cup Arborio rice
- 1/2 cup dry white wine
- 3 cups chicken or vegetable broth
- 1/4 cup grated Parmesan cheese

- 1 lb (450g) fresh scallops
- 2 tbsp butter
- 1 shallot, finely chopped
- 2 cloves garlic, minced
- 1/4 cup heavy cream
- Salt and pepper to taste
- Fresh chives, chopped, for garnish

Directions:

1. Preheat the sous vide water bath to 135°F (57°C).
2. Season the scallops with salt and pepper and place them in a vacuum-sealed bag.
3. In a separate large bowl, combine Arborio rice and dry white wine.
4. In a medium saucepan, sauté shallots and garlic in butter until translucent. Add the rice-wine mixture and stir.
5. Slowly add the chicken or vegetable broth, 1/2 cup at a time, while stirring constantly until the rice is cooked and creamy.
6. In the last 10 minutes of cooking the rice, add the sous vide scallops to the water bath and cook for 10 minutes.
7. Once the risotto and scallops are done, remove the scallops from the bag and add them to the risotto along with the heavy cream and grated Parmesan cheese. Stir to combine.
8. Serve the scallop risotto garnished with fresh chives.

Nutrition: Calories: 420kcal; Fat: 16g; Carb: 40g; Protein: 26g

35. Chilean Sea Bass with Ginger Soy Glaze

Preparation Time: 10 minutes

Cooking Time: 1 hour and 15 minutes

Servings: 2

Ingredients:

- 2 Chilean sea bass fillets
- 2 tbsp soy sauce
- 1 tbsp honey
- 1 tbsp rice vinegar
- 1 tbsp fresh ginger, grated
- 1 garlic clove, minced
- 1 green onion, thinly sliced

Directions:

1. Preheat the sous vide water bath to 130°F (54°C).
2. In a bowl, mix soy sauce, honey, rice vinegar, grated ginger, and minced garlic to make the glaze.

3. Pat the sea bass fillets dry and place them in separate vacuum-sealed bags.

4. Pour the glaze over the fish, ensuring they are coated evenly.

5. Seal the bags and cook in the sous vide water bath for 1 hour and 15 minutes.

6. Once done, remove the sea bass from the bags, garnish with sliced green onions, and serve.

Nutrition: Calories: 340kcal; Fat: 8g; Carb: 16g; Protein: 45g

36. Octopus Salad

Preparation Time: 15 minutes

Cooking Time: 3 hours

Servings: 4

Ingredients:

- 1 lb (450g) octopus tentacles
- 1 lemon, juiced
- 2 tbsp olive oil
- 2 cloves garlic, minced
- 1/2 tsp smoked paprika
- 1/4 tsp cayenne pepper (optional)
- Salt and pepper to taste
- Mixed greens for serving

Directions:

1. Preheat the sous vide water bath to 170°F (77°C).

2. Rinse the octopus tentacles under cold water and pat them dry.

3. Place the tentacles in a vacuum-sealed bag and add lemon juice, olive oil, minced garlic, smoked paprika, cayenne pepper (if using), salt, and pepper.

4. Seal the bag and cook in the sous vide water bath for 3 hours.

5. Once done, remove the octopus from the bag and grill or sear briefly to get a charred texture.

6. Serve the sous vide octopus on a bed of mixed greens.

Nutrition: Calories: 220kcal; Fat: 12g; Carb: 4g; Protein: 24g

37. Tuna Steaks with Sesame Ginger Glaze

Preparation Time: 10 minutes

Cooking Time: 1 hour and 30 minutes

Servings: 2

Ingredients:

- 2 tuna steaks
- 3 tbsp soy sauce
- 1 tbsp sesame oil

- 1 tbsp rice vinegar
- 1 tbsp honey
- 1 tbsp fresh ginger, grated
- 1 garlic clove, minced
- 1 tsp sesame seeds
- Green onions, thinly sliced, for garnish

Directions:

1. Preheat the sous vide water bath to 120°F (49°C) for rare doneness or 130°F (54°C) for medium-rare doneness.
2. In a bowl, mix soy sauce, sesame oil, rice vinegar, honey, grated ginger, minced garlic, and sesame seeds to make the glaze.
3. Pat the tuna steaks dry and place them in separate vacuum-sealed bags.
4. Pour the glaze over the steaks, ensuring they are coated evenly.
5. Seal the bags and cook in the sous vide water bath for 1 hour and 30 minutes.
6. Once done, remove the tuna steaks from the bags, garnish with sliced green onions, and serve.

Nutrition: Calories: 380kcal; Fat: 12g; Carb: 14g; Protein: 48g

38. Halibut with Lemon Caper Sauce

Preparation Time: 15 minutes

Cooking Time: 1 hour and 15 minutes

Servings: 2

Ingredients:

- 2 halibut fillets
- 2 tbsp olive oil
- 2 tbsp lemon juice
- 2 tbsp capers, drained
- 1/4 cup white wine
- 1/4 cup chicken or vegetable broth
- 2 tbsp butter
- Salt and pepper to taste
- Fresh parsley, chopped, for garnish

Directions:

1. Preheat the sous vide water bath to 130°F (54°C).
2. Season the halibut fillets with salt and pepper and place them in separate vacuum-sealed bags.
3. Pour olive oil and lemon juice over the fish in the bags.
4. Seal the bags and cook in the sous vide water bath for 1 hour.

5. In a saucepan over medium heat, combine capers, white wine, and chicken or vegetable broth. Simmer until the liquid reduces by half.

6. Remove the saucepan from the heat and whisk in butter to create a creamy lemon caper sauce.

7. Once the halibut is done, remove it from the bags and serve with the lemon caper sauce drizzled over it. Garnish with chopped fresh parsley.

Nutrition: Calories: 450kcal; Fat: 28g; Carb: 4g; Protein: 40g

39. Cajun Catfish Fillets

Preparation Time: 10 minutes

Cooking Time: 1 hour and 30 minutes

Servings: 4

Ingredients:

- 4 catfish fillets
- 2 tbsp Cajun seasoning
- 1 lemon, thinly sliced
- 2 tbsp olive oil
- Salt and pepper to taste

Directions:

1. Preheat the sous vide water bath to 135°F (57°C).

2. Season the catfish fillets with Cajun seasoning, salt, and pepper and place them in separate vacuum-sealed bags.

3. Add lemon slices and a drizzle of olive oil to each bag.

4. Seal the bags and cook in the sous vide water bath for 1 hour and 30 minutes.

5. Once done, remove the catfish from the bags and sear briefly in a hot skillet for added texture and flavor.

Nutrition: Calories: 240kcal; Fat: 14g; Carb: 4g; Protein: 26g

40. Garlic Herb Scallops

Preparation Time: 10 minutes

Cooking Time: 40 minutes

Servings: 2

Ingredients:

- 1 lb (450g) sea scallops
- 3 tbsp olive oil
- 4 cloves garlic, minced
- 2 tbsp fresh thyme, chopped
- 2 tbsp fresh parsley, chopped

- Salt and pepper to taste

Directions:

1. Preheat the sous vide water bath to 125°F (52°C) for medium-rare doneness or 135°F (57°C) for medium doneness.
2. In a bowl, mix olive oil, minced garlic, chopped thyme, chopped parsley, salt, and pepper.
3. Place the scallops in a vacuum-sealed bag and pour the garlic herb mixture over them.
4. Seal the bag and cook in the sous vide water bath for 40 minutes.
5. Once done, remove the scallops from the bag and serve immediately.

Nutrition: Calories: 300kcal; Fat: 16g; Carb: 6g; Protein: 30g

41. Lemon Herb Cod

Preparation Time: 10 minutes

Cooking Time: 1 hour and 15 minutes

Servings: 2

Ingredients:

- 2 cod fillets
- 2 tbsp olive oil
- 2 tbsp lemon juice
- 2 cloves garlic, minced
- 1 tsp dried oregano
- 1 tsp dried thyme
- 1 tsp dried rosemary
- Salt and pepper to taste

Directions:

1. Preheat the sous vide water bath to 125°F (52°C) for medium-rare doneness or 135°F (57°C) for medium doneness.
2. In a bowl, mix olive oil, lemon juice, minced garlic, dried oregano, dried thyme, dried rosemary, salt, and pepper.
3. Place the cod fillets in separate vacuum-sealed bags and pour the lemon herb mixture over them.
4. Seal the bags and cook in the sous vide water bath for 1 hour and 15 minutes.
5. Once done, remove the cod fillets from the bags and serve.

Nutrition: Calories: 280kcal; Fat: 12g; Carb: 4g; Protein: 30g

42. Tarragon Lobster Tails

Preparation Time: 20 minutes

Cooking Time: 40 minutes

Servings: 2

Ingredients:

- 2 lobster tails
- 2 tbsp olive oil
- 2 tbsp fresh tarragon, chopped
- 2 cloves garlic, minced
- 2 tsp lemon zest
- Salt and pepper to taste

Directions:

1. Preheat the sous vide water bath to 140°F (60°C).
2. Butterfly the lobster tails by cutting the top shell lengthwise and carefully pulling the meat upward.
3. In a bowl, mix olive oil, chopped tarragon, minced garlic, lemon zest, salt, and pepper.
4. Place each lobster tail in a separate vacuum-sealed bag and pour the tarragon mixture over them.
5. Seal the bags and cook in the sous vide water bath for 40 minutes.
6. Once done, remove the lobster tails from the bags and serve.

Nutrition: Calories: 260kcal; Fat: 14g; Carb: 2g; Protein: 30g

43. Smoked Paprika Prawns

Preparation Time: 15 minutes

Cooking Time: 30 minutes

Servings: 4

Ingredients:

- 1 lb (450g) large prawns, peeled and deveined
- 3 tbsp olive oil
- 2 tsp smoked paprika
- 1 tsp garlic powder
- 1 tsp onion powder
- 1/2 tsp cayenne pepper (optional)
- Salt and pepper to taste

Directions:

1. Preheat the sous vide water bath to 130°F (54°C) for medium-rare doneness or 140°F (60°C) for medium doneness.
2. In a bowl, mix olive oil, smoked paprika, garlic powder, onion powder, cayenne pepper (if using), salt, and pepper.
3. Place the cleaned prawns in a vacuum-sealed bag and pour the smoked paprika mixture over them.
4. Seal the bag and cook in the sous vide water bath for 30 minutes.
5. Once done, remove the prawns from the bag and serve immediately.

Nutrition: Calories: 180kcal; Fat: 10g; Carb: 2g; Protein: 20g

44. Coconut Lime Tilapia

Preparation Time: 10 minutes

Cooking Time: 1 hour

Servings: 4

Ingredients:

- 4 tilapia fillets
- 1/2 cup coconut milk
- 2 tbsp lime juice
- 1 tsp lime zest
- 2 tbsp fresh cilantro, chopped
- 1 tsp ground cumin
- 1/2 tsp turmeric
- Salt and pepper to taste

Directions:

1. Preheat the sous vide water bath to 125°F (52°C) for medium-rare doneness or 135°F (57°C) for medium doneness.
2. In a bowl, mix coconut milk, lime juice, lime zest, chopped cilantro, ground cumin, turmeric, salt, and pepper.
3. Place the tilapia fillets in separate vacuum-sealed bags and pour the coconut lime mixture over them.
4. Seal the bags and cook in the sous vide water bath for 1 hour.
5. Once done, remove the tilapia fillets from the bags and serve.

Nutrition: Calories: 220kcal; Fat: 10g; Carb: 4g; Protein: 26g

45. Mediterranean Swordfish

Preparation Time: 15 minutes

Cooking Time: 1 hour and 30 minutes

Servings: 2

Ingredients:

- 2 swordfish steaks
- 3 tbsp olive oil
- 2 tbsp lemon juice
- 2 cloves garlic, minced
- 1 tbsp fresh oregano, chopped
- 1 tbsp fresh basil, chopped
- 1 tbsp fresh parsley, chopped
- Salt and pepper to taste

Directions:

1. Preheat the sous vide water bath to 130°F (54°C).
2. Season the swordfish steaks with salt and pepper and place them in separate vacuum-sealed bags.
3. In a bowl, mix olive oil, lemon juice, minced garlic, chopped oregano, chopped basil, and chopped parsley.
4. Pour the olive oil mixture over the swordfish steaks in the bags.
5. Seal the bags and cook in the sous vide water bath for 1 hour and 30 minutes.
6. Once done, remove the swordfish steaks from the bags and serve.

Nutrition: Calories: 380kcal; Fat: 24g; Carb: 4g; Protein: 40g

Chapter 6. Poultry

46. Chicken Breast with Lemon Herb Sauce

Preparation Time: 10 minutes

Cooking Time: 1 hour

Servings: 4

Ingredients:

- 4 boneless, skinless chicken breasts
- 2 tablespoons olive oil
- 2 garlic cloves, minced
- 1 lemon, juiced and zested
- 1 teaspoon dried thyme
- 1 teaspoon dried rosemary
- Salt and pepper to taste

Directions:

1. Preheat the sous vide water bath to 145°F (63°C).
2. Season the chicken breasts with salt and pepper.
3. Place the chicken breasts in a sous vide bag and add olive oil, garlic, lemon juice, lemon zest, thyme, and rosemary.
4. Seal the bag using the water displacement method and cook in the water bath for 1 hour.
5. Remove the chicken from the bag and sear in a hot skillet for 1-2 minutes on each side.
6. Serve with the lemon herb sauce made from the juices in the bag.

Nutrition: Calories: 250kcal; Fat: 12g; Carb: 4g; Protein: 30g

47. Turkey Breast with Cranberry Glaze

Preparation Time: 15 minutes

Cooking Time: 3 hours

Servings: 6

Ingredients:

- 1 (3-pound) turkey breast
- 1 cup cranberry sauce
- 1/4 cup balsamic vinegar
- 2 tablespoons honey
- 1 teaspoon dried sage

- Salt and pepper to taste

Directions:

1. Preheat the sous vide water bath to 150°F (66°C).
2. Season the turkey breast with salt, pepper, and dried sage.
3. Place the turkey breast in a sous vide bag.
4. In a separate bowl, mix cranberry sauce, balsamic vinegar, and honey.
5. Pour the cranberry glaze into the bag with the turkey breast and seal using the water displacement method.
6. Cook in the water bath for 3 hours.
7. Remove the turkey from the bag and brush with additional glaze.
8. Broil the turkey in the oven for 3-5 minutes until the glaze caramelizes.

Nutrition: Calories: 350kcal; Fat: 8g; Carb: 25g; Protein: 40g

48. Duck Breast with Orange Sauce

Preparation Time: 20 minutes

Cooking Time: 2 hours

Servings: 2

Ingredients:

- 2 duck breasts
- Zest of 1 orange
- Juice of 2 oranges
- 2 tablespoons soy sauce
- 2 tablespoons honey
- 1 tablespoon grated ginger
- 2 garlic cloves, minced
- Salt and pepper to taste

Directions:

1. Preheat the sous vide water bath to 135°F (57°C).
2. Season the duck breasts with salt and pepper.
3. In a bowl, mix orange zest, orange juice, soy sauce, honey, grated ginger, and minced garlic.
4. Place the duck breasts in a sous vide bag and pour the orange sauce over them.
5. Seal the bag using the water displacement method and cook in the water bath for 2 hours.
6. Remove the duck from the bag and sear in a hot skillet for 2-3 minutes on each side.
7. Serve with additional orange sauce.

Nutrition: Calories: 400kcal; Fat: 20g; Carb: 30g; Protein: 25g

49. Chicken Thighs with Garlic Butter

Preparation Time: 10 minutes

Cooking Time: 2 hours

Servings: 4

Ingredients:

- 8 bone-in, skin-on chicken thighs
- 4 tablespoons butter
- 4 garlic cloves, minced
- 1 tablespoon chopped fresh parsley
- Salt and pepper to taste

Directions:

1. Preheat the sous vide water bath to 165°F (74°C).
2. Season the chicken thighs with salt and pepper.
3. In a small saucepan, melt the butter and add minced garlic. Cook until fragrant.
4. Place the chicken thighs in a sous vide bag and pour the garlic butter over them.
5. Seal the bag using the water displacement method and cook in the water bath for 2 hours.
6. Remove the chicken from the bag and sear in a hot skillet for 2-3 minutes on each side.
7. Sprinkle with chopped parsley before serving.

Nutrition: Calories: 400kcal; Fat: 30g; Carb: 2g; Protein: 30g

50. Cornish Hens with Herb Rub

Preparation Time: 15 minutes

Cooking Time: 3 hours

Servings: 2

Ingredients:

- 2 Cornish hens
- 2 tablespoons olive oil
- 1 tablespoon chopped fresh thyme
- 1 tablespoon chopped fresh rosemary
- 1 tablespoon chopped fresh sage
- Salt and pepper to taste

Directions:

1. Preheat the sous vide water bath to 155°F (68°C).
2. Season the Cornish hens with salt and pepper.
3. In a bowl, mix olive oil, chopped thyme, rosemary, and sage.
4. Rub the herb mixture over the Cornish hens.

5. Place each hen in a separate sous vide bag and seal using the water displacement method.
6. Cook in the water bath for 3 hours.
7. Remove the hens from the bags and sear in a hot skillet for 3-4 minutes on each side.

Nutrition: Calories: 500kcal; Fat: 30g; Carb: 0g; Protein: 40g

51. Chicken Wings with Buffalo Sauce

Preparation Time: 10 minutes

Cooking Time: 2 hours

Servings: 6

Ingredients:

- 24 chicken wings
- 1/2 cup hot sauce
- 1/4 cup melted butter
- 1 tablespoon Worcestershire sauce
- 1 tablespoon apple cider vinegar
- Salt and pepper to taste

Directions:

Preheat the sous vide water bath to 165°F (74°C).

Season the chicken wings with salt and pepper.

In a bowl, mix hot sauce, melted butter, Worcestershire sauce, and apple cider vinegar.

Place the chicken wings in a sous vide bag and pour the buffalo sauce over them.

Seal the bag using the water displacement method and cook in the water bath for 2 hours.

Remove the wings from the bag and broil in the oven for 5-7 minutes until crispy.

Nutrition: Calories: 450kcal; Fat: 30g; Carb: 5g; Protein: 30g

52. Chicken Fajitas

Preparation Time: 15 minutes

Cooking Time: 2 hours

Servings: 4

Ingredients:

- 1 pound chicken breast, sliced
- 1 bell pepper, sliced
- 1 onion, sliced
- 2 tablespoons fajita seasoning
- 2 tablespoons olive oil
- 2 tablespoons lime juice
- Salt and pepper to taste

- Tortillas and desired toppings for serving

Directions:

1. Preheat the sous vide water bath to 150°F (66°C).
2. Season the sliced chicken breast with fajita seasoning, salt, and pepper.
3. In a bowl, mix olive oil and lime juice.
4. Place the chicken, bell pepper, and onion in a sous vide bag and pour the olive oil mixture over them.
5. Seal the bag using the water displacement method and cook in the water bath for 2 hours.
6. Remove the contents from the bag and sauté in a hot skillet until lightly browned.
7. Serve the fajita mixture with warm tortillas and your favorite toppings.

Nutrition: Calories: 350kcal; Fat: 15g; Carb: 25g; Protein: 25g

53. Chicken Parmesan

Preparation Time: 20 minutes

Cooking Time: 2 hours

Servings: 4

Ingredients:

- 4 boneless, skinless chicken breasts
- 1 cup marinara sauce
- 1 cup shredded mozzarella cheese
- 1/2 cup grated Parmesan cheese
- 1/2 cup breadcrumbs
- 2 eggs, beaten
- Salt and pepper to taste
- Fresh basil leaves for garnish

Directions:

1. Preheat the sous vide water bath to 150°F (66°C).
2. Season the chicken breasts with salt and pepper.
3. Place the chicken breasts in a sous vide bag and cook in the water bath for 2 hours.
4. Preheat the oven to 400°F (200°C).
5. Remove the chicken from the bag and pat dry with paper towels.
6. Dip each chicken breast into the beaten eggs and then coat with breadcrumbs.
7. Place the chicken on a baking sheet and top each breast with marinara sauce, mozzarella, and Parmesan cheese.
8. Bake in the oven for 10-12 minutes or until the cheese is bubbly and golden.
9. Garnish with fresh basil leaves before serving.

Nutrition: Calories: 450kcal; Fat: 15g; Carb: 40g; Protein: 40g

54. Chicken Teriyaki

Preparation Time: 10 minutes

Cooking Time: 2 hours

Servings: 4

Ingredients:

- 4 boneless, skinless chicken thighs
- 1/2 cup soy sauce
- 1/4 cup mirin
- 2 tablespoons honey
- 1 tablespoon sesame oil
- 2 garlic cloves, minced
- 1 teaspoon grated ginger
- Sesame seeds and green onions for garnish

Directions:

1. Preheat the sous vide water bath to 165°F (74°C).
2. Season the chicken thighs with salt and pepper.
3. In a bowl, mix soy sauce, mirin, honey, sesame oil, minced garlic, and grated ginger.
4. Place the chicken thighs in a sous vide bag and pour the teriyaki sauce over them.
5. Seal the bag using the water displacement method and cook in the water bath for 2 hours.
6. Remove the chicken from the bag and sear in a hot skillet for 2-3 minutes on each side.
7. Garnish with sesame seeds and chopped green onions before serving.

Nutrition: Calories: 350kcal; Fat: 15g; Carb: 20g; Protein: 30g

55. Chicken Curry

Preparation Time: 15 minutes

Cooking Time: 4 hours

Servings: 4

Ingredients:

- 4 chicken thighs, bone-in, skin-on
- 1 cup coconut milk
- 2 tablespoons red curry paste
- 1 tablespoon fish sauce
- 1 tablespoon brown sugar
- 1 tablespoon lime juice
- 1 bell pepper, sliced
- 1 onion, sliced

- Fresh cilantro for garnish

Directions:

1. Preheat the sous vide water bath to 165°F (74°C).
2. Season the chicken thighs with salt and pepper.
3. In a bowl, mix coconut milk, red curry paste, fish sauce, brown sugar, and lime juice.
4. Place the chicken thighs, bell pepper, and onion in a sous vide bag and pour the curry mixture over them.
5. Seal the bag using the water displacement method and cook in the water bath for 4 hours.
6. Remove the chicken from the bag and sear in a hot skillet for 2-3 minutes on each side.
7. Serve the chicken with the curry sauce and garnish with fresh cilantro.

Nutrition: Calories: 400kcal; Fat: 25g; Carb: 15g; Protein: 25g

56. Chicken Alfredo Pasta

Preparation Time: 15 minutes

Cooking Time: 2 hours

Servings: 4

Ingredients:

- 2 boneless, skinless chicken breasts
- 1 cup heavy cream
- 1/2 cup grated Parmesan cheese
- 2 garlic cloves, minced
- 2 tablespoons butter
- 2 tablespoons chopped fresh parsley
- Salt and pepper to taste
- Cooked fettuccine pasta for serving

Directions:

1. Preheat the sous vide water bath to 150°F (66°C).
2. Season the chicken breasts with salt and pepper.
3. Place the chicken breasts in a sous vide bag and cook in the water bath for 2 hours.
4. In a saucepan, melt the butter and add minced garlic. Cook until fragrant.
5. Add heavy cream and grated Parmesan cheese to the saucepan, stirring until the cheese melts and the sauce thickens.
6. Remove the chicken from the bag and slice.
7. Toss the cooked fettuccine pasta with the Alfredo sauce and serve with sliced chicken on top.
8. Garnish with chopped parsley before serving.

Nutrition: Calories: 600kcal; Fat: 40g; Carb: 20g; Protein: 40g

57. Turkey Legs with BBQ Glaze

Preparation Time: 10 minutes

Cooking Time: 4 hours

Servings: 4

Ingredients:

- 4 turkey legs
- 1 cup barbecue sauce
- 1/4 cup apple cider vinegar
- 2 tablespoons brown sugar
- 1 teaspoon smoked paprika
- Salt and pepper to taste

Directions:

1. Preheat the sous vide water bath to 150°F (66°C).
2. Season the turkey legs with salt, pepper, and smoked paprika.
3. In a bowl, mix barbecue sauce, apple cider vinegar, and brown sugar.
4. Place the turkey legs in a sous vide bag and pour the BBQ sauce mixture over them.
5. Seal the bag using the water displacement method and cook in the water bath for
6. 4 hours.
7. Remove the turkey legs from the bag and sear on a hot grill or under the broiler for 2-3 minutes on each side.

Nutrition: Calories: 550kcal; Fat: 20g; Carb: 40g; Protein: 40g

58. Chicken and Vegetable Stir-Fry

Preparation Time: 20 minutes

Cooking Time: 2 hours

Servings: 4

Ingredients:

- 1 pound chicken breast, sliced
- 1 cup broccoli florets
- 1 cup sliced carrots
- 1 cup sliced bell peppers
- 1/2 cup soy sauce
- 2 tablespoons honey
- 1 tablespoon sesame oil
- 2 garlic cloves, minced
- 1 teaspoon grated ginger

- 2 green onions, sliced
- Sesame seeds for garnish

Directions:

1. Preheat the sous vide water bath to 150°F (66°C).
2. Season the chicken breast with salt and pepper.
3. In a bowl, mix soy sauce, honey, sesame oil, minced garlic, and grated ginger.
4. Place the chicken, broccoli, carrots, and bell peppers in a sous vide bag and pour the sauce over them.
5. Seal the bag using the water displacement method and cook in the water bath for 2 hours.
6. Remove the contents from the bag and sauté in a hot skillet until the vegetables are tender and the chicken is cooked through.
7. Garnish with sliced green onions and sesame seeds before serving.

Nutrition: Calories: 350kcal; Fat: 10g; Carb: 30g; Protein: 30g

59. Chicken Caesar Salad

Preparation Time: 15 minutes

Cooking Time: 2 hours

Servings: 4

Ingredients:

- 2 boneless, skinless chicken breasts
- 1 tablespoon olive oil
- 1 tablespoon lemon juice
- 1 teaspoon Dijon mustard
- 2 garlic cloves, minced
- Salt and pepper to taste
- Romaine lettuce
- Croutons
- Grated Parmesan cheese
- Caesar dressing for serving

Directions:

1. Preheat the sous vide water bath to 150°F (66°C).
2. Season the chicken breasts with salt and pepper.
3. In a bowl, mix olive oil, lemon juice, Dijon mustard, and minced garlic.
4. Place the chicken breasts in a sous vide bag and pour the dressing over them.
5. Seal the bag using the water displacement method and cook in the water bath for 2 hours.
6. Remove the chicken from the bag and slice.
7. Arrange romaine lettuce on plates and top with sliced chicken, croutons, and grated Parmesan cheese.
8. Drizzle Caesar dressing over the salad before serving.

Nutrition: Calories: 300kcal; Fat: 15g; Carb: 15g; Protein: 25g

60. Piri Piri Chicken

Preparation Time: 10 minutes

Cooking Time: 2 hours

Servings: 4

Ingredients:

- 4 bone-in, skin-on chicken thighs
- 2 tablespoons olive oil
- 2 tablespoons lemon juice
- 1 tablespoon paprika
- 1 tablespoon chili powder
- 1 teaspoon dried oregano
- 1 teaspoon dried thyme
- Salt and pepper to taste

Directions:

1. Preheat the sous vide water bath to 165°F (74°C).
2. Season the chicken thighs with salt and pepper.
3. In a bowl, mix olive oil, lemon juice, paprika, chili powder, dried oregano, and dried thyme.
4. Place the chicken thighs in a sous vide bag and pour the Piri Piri sauce over them.
5. Seal the bag using the water displacement method and cook in the water bath for 2 hours.
6. Remove the chicken from the bag and sear in a hot skillet for 2-3 minutes on each side.

Nutrition: Calories: 400kcal; Fat: 25g; Carb: 5g; Protein: 30g

Chapter 7. Meat

61. Ribeye Steak

Preparation Time: 10 minutes

Cooking Time: 2 hours

Servings: 2

Ingredients:

- 2 ribeye steaks (1-inch thick)
- 2 tablespoons olive oil
- 2 garlic cloves, minced
- 1 tablespoon fresh thyme leaves
- Salt and pepper to taste

Directions:

1. Preheat the sous vide water bath to 130°F (54°C).
2. Season the steaks with salt, pepper, minced garlic, and thyme. Drizzle with olive oil.
3. Place the seasoned steaks in a vacuum-sealed bag and seal.
4. Cook the steaks in the water bath for 2 hours.
5. Remove the steaks from the bag and pat dry with paper towels.
6. Sear the steaks on a hot grill or pan for 1-2 minutes per side.
7. Serve and enjoy!

Nutrition: Calories: 400kcal; Fat: 28g; Carb: 0g; Protein: 35g

62. Salmon

Preparation Time: 5 minutes

Cooking Time: 1 hour

Servings: 4

Ingredients:

- 4 salmon fillets
- 2 tablespoons soy sauce
- 2 tablespoons honey
- 1 tablespoon lemon juice
- 1 teaspoon grated ginger
- Salt and pepper to taste

Directions:

1. Set the sous vide water bath to 130°F (54°C).
2. In a bowl, mix soy sauce, honey, lemon juice, grated ginger, salt, and pepper.
3. Place the salmon fillets in a vacuum-sealed bag and pour the marinade over them. Seal the bag.
4. Cook the salmon in the water bath for 1 hour.
5. Remove the salmon from the bag and sear briefly in a hot pan.
6. Serve with your favorite side dishes.

Nutrition: Calories: 250kcal; Fat: 12g; Carb: 8g; Protein: 30g

63. Chicken Breast

Preparation Time: 10 minutes

Cooking Time: 2 hours

Servings: 3

Ingredients:

- 3 boneless, skinless chicken breasts
- 2 tablespoons olive oil
- 2 garlic cloves, minced
- 1 tablespoon fresh rosemary, chopped
- Salt and pepper to taste

Directions:

1. Preheat the sous vide water bath to 150°F (66°C).
2. Season the chicken breasts with salt, pepper, minced garlic, and chopped rosemary. Drizzle with olive oil.
3. Place the chicken breasts in a vacuum-sealed bag and seal.
4. Cook the chicken in the water bath for 2 hours.
5. Remove the chicken from the bag and pat dry with paper towels.
6. Sear the chicken on a hot grill or pan for 1-2 minutes per side.
7. Serve with your favorite side dishes.

Nutrition: Calories: 220kcal; Fat: 10g; Carb: 1g; Protein: 30g

64. Pork Tenderloin

Preparation Time: 15 minutes

Cooking Time: 3 hours

Servings: 4

Ingredients:

- 1 pork tenderloin (about 1 lb)
- 2 tablespoons olive oil

- 2 tablespoons balsamic vinegar
- 1 tablespoon Dijon mustard
- 1 teaspoon dried thyme
- Salt and pepper to taste

Directions:

1. Preheat the sous vide water bath to 140°F (60°C).
2. In a bowl, mix olive oil, balsamic vinegar, Dijon mustard, dried thyme, salt, and pepper.
3. Place the pork tenderloin in a vacuum-sealed bag and pour the marinade over it. Seal the bag.
4. Cook the pork in the water bath for 3 hours.
5. Remove the pork from the bag and pat dry with paper towels.
6. Sear the pork on a hot grill or pan for 1-2 minutes per side.
7. Slice and serve.

Nutrition: Calories: 250kcal; Fat: 10g; Carb: 2g; Protein: 30g

65. Duck Breast

Preparation Time: 10 minutes

Cooking Time: 2 hours

Servings: 2

Ingredients:

- 2 duck breasts
- 2 tablespoons orange juice
- 2 tablespoons soy sauce
- 1 tablespoon honey
- 1 teaspoon Chinese five-spice powder
- Salt and pepper to taste

Directions:

1. Set the sous vide water bath to 135°F (57°C).
2. Mix orange juice, soy sauce, honey, Chinese five-spice powder, salt, and pepper in a bowl.
3. Score the duck skin and place the breasts in a vacuum-sealed bag. Pour the marinade over them and seal the bag.
4. Cook the duck breasts in the water bath for 2 hours.
5. Remove the duck from the bag and pat dry with paper towels.
6. Sear the duck skin-side down in a hot pan until crispy.
7. Slice and serve with your favorite side dishes.

Nutrition: Calories: 350kcal; Fat: 28g; Carb: 8g; Protein: 25g

66. Lamb Chops

Preparation Time: 10 minutes

Cooking Time: 2 hours

Servings: 2

Ingredients:

- 4 lamb chops
- 2 tablespoons olive oil
- 2 garlic cloves, minced
- 1 tablespoon fresh rosemary, chopped
- Salt and pepper to taste

Directions:

1. Preheat the sous vide water bath to 140°F (60°C).
2. Season the lamb chops with salt, pepper, minced garlic, and chopped rosemary. Drizzle with olive oil.
3. Place the seasoned lamb chops in a vacuum-sealed bag and seal.
4. Cook the lamb in the water bath for 2 hours.
5. Remove the lamb chops from the bag and pat dry with paper towels.
6. Sear the lamb chops on a hot grill or pan for 1-2 minutes per side.
7. Serve with mint sauce or your favorite sauce.

Nutrition: Calories: 400kcal; Fat: 30g; Carb: 1g; Protein: 30g

67. Turkey Breast

Preparation Time: 10 minutes

Cooking Time: 3 hours

Servings: 4

Ingredients:

- 1 boneless turkey breast (about 2 lbs)
- 2 tablespoons olive oil
- 1 tablespoon smoked paprika
- 1 teaspoon dried thyme
- Salt and pepper to taste

Directions:

1. Preheat the sous vide water bath to 150°F (66°C).
2. Rub the turkey breast with olive oil, smoked paprika, dried thyme, salt, and pepper.
3. Place the turkey breast in a vacuum-sealed bag and seal.
4. Cook the turkey in the water bath for 3 hours.
5. Remove the turkey from the bag and pat dry with paper towels.

6. Sear the turkey on a hot grill or pan for 1-2 minutes per side.

7. Slice and serve with cranberry sauce or gravy.

Nutrition: Calories: 200kcal; Fat: 8g; Carb: 2g; Protein: 30g

68. Pork Ribs

Preparation Time: 15 minutes

Cooking Time: 24 hours

Servings: 4

Ingredients:

- 2 racks of pork ribs
- 1 cup BBQ sauce
- 1/4 cup apple cider vinegar
- 1 tablespoon smoked paprika
- 1 tablespoon brown sugar
- Salt and pepper to taste

Directions:

1. Preheat the sous vide water bath to 165°F (74°C).

2. Season the pork ribs with salt, pepper, smoked paprika, and brown sugar.

3. In a bowl, mix the BBQ sauce and apple cider vinegar.

4. Place each rack of ribs in a separate vacuum-sealed bag and pour half of the BBQ sauce mixture into each bag. Seal the bags.

5. Cook the ribs in the water bath for 24 hours.

6. Preheat your grill to medium-high heat.

7. Remove the ribs from the bags and brush with additional BBQ sauce.

8. Grill the ribs for 5-10 minutes on each side, basting with more BBQ sauce as needed.

9. Serve and enjoy!

Nutrition: Calories: 500kcal; Fat: 30g; Carb: 20g; Protein: 35g

69. Corned Beef Brisket

Preparation Time: 15 minutes

Cooking Time: 48 hours

Servings: 6

Ingredients:

- 3 lbs corned beef brisket
- 1 tablespoon pickling spices
- 4 garlic cloves, minced
- 2 tablespoons brown sugar

- Salt and pepper to taste

Directions:

1. Preheat the sous vide water bath to 140°F (60°C).
2. Rinse the corned beef brisket under cold water and pat dry with paper towels.
3. Rub the brisket with pickling spices, minced garlic, brown sugar, salt, and pepper.
4. Place the brisket in a vacuum-sealed bag and seal.
5. Cook the brisket in the water bath for 48 hours.
6. Preheat your oven to 375°F (190°C).
7. Remove the brisket from the bag and place it on a baking sheet lined with aluminum foil.
8. Roast the brisket in the oven for 20-30 minutes until it develops a crust.
9. Slice and serve with mustard or sauerkraut.

Nutrition: Calories: 400kcal; Fat: 25g; Carb: 5g; Protein: 35g

70. Veal Cutlets

Preparation Time: 10 minutes

Cooking Time: 1 hour

Servings: 4

Ingredients:

- 4 veal cutlets
- 1 cup breadcrumbs
- 1/2 cup grated Parmesan cheese
- 2 eggs, beaten
- 1 tablespoon Italian seasoning
- Salt and pepper to taste

Directions:

1. Set the sous vide water bath to 140°F (60°C).
2. In a shallow bowl, mix breadcrumbs, grated Parmesan cheese, Italian seasoning, salt, and pepper.
3. Dip each veal cutlet into beaten eggs, then coat with the breadcrumb mixture.
4. Place the breaded veal cutlets in a vacuum-sealed bag and seal.
5. Cook the cutlets in the water bath for 1 hour.
6. Preheat a skillet with olive oil over medium-high heat.
7. Remove the cutlets from the bag and sear for 1-2 minutes per side until golden brown.
8. Serve with lemon wedges and your favorite vegetables.

Nutrition: Calories: 300kcal; Fat: 15g; Carb: 10g; Protein: 30g

71. Quail

Preparation Time: 10 minutes

Cooking Time: 2 hours

Servings: 4

Ingredients:

- 4 quail, cleaned and gutted
- 2 tablespoons olive oil
- 1 tablespoon fresh thyme leaves
- 1 tablespoon fresh rosemary, chopped
- Salt and pepper to taste

Directions:

1. Preheat the sous vide water bath to 145°F (63°C).
2. Season the quail with salt, pepper, fresh thyme leaves, and chopped rosemary. Drizzle with olive oil.
3. Place the seasoned quail in a vacuum-sealed bag and seal.
4. Cook the quail in the water bath for 2 hours.
5. Remove the quail from the bag and pat dry with paper towels.
6. Sear the quail on a hot grill or pan for 1-2 minutes per side.
7. Serve with a side salad or roasted vegetables.

Nutrition: Calories: 200kcal; Fat: 10g; Carb: 0g; Protein: 25g

72. Lobster Tail

Preparation Time: 5 minutes

Cooking Time: 45 minutes

Servings: 2

Ingredients:

- 2 lobster tails
- 1/4 cup butter, melted
- 2 garlic cloves, minced
- 1 tablespoon fresh parsley, chopped
- Salt and pepper to taste

Directions:

1. Set the sous vide water bath to 140°F (60°C).
2. In a bowl, mix melted butter, minced garlic, chopped parsley, salt, and pepper.
3. Using kitchen shears, cut the top shell of each lobster tail down the center to expose the meat.
4. Place the lobster tails in a vacuum-sealed bag and pour the butter mixture over them. Seal the bag.
5. Cook the lobster in the water bath for 45 minutes.
6. Preheat your grill to medium-high heat.
7. Remove the lobster tails from the bag and place them directly on the grill.
8. Grill the lobster tails for 2-3 minutes per side, basting with more butter mixture.

9. Serve with lemon wedges and enjoy!

Nutrition: Calories: 300kcal; Fat: 15g; Carb: 2g; Protein: 40g

73. Duck Confit

Preparation Time: 15 minutes

Cooking Time: 12 hours

Servings: 4

Ingredients:

- 4 duck legs
- 4 cloves garlic, crushed
- 4 sprigs fresh thyme
- 4 sprigs fresh rosemary
- 2 tablespoons duck fat (or olive oil)
- Salt and pepper to taste

Directions:

1. Preheat the sous vide water bath to 165°F (74°C).
2. Season the duck legs with salt and pepper.
3. Place each duck leg in a separate vacuum-sealed bag and add crushed garlic, fresh thyme, and fresh rosemary to each bag. Add a tablespoon of duck fat or olive oil to each bag. Seal the bags.
4. Cook the duck legs in the water bath for 12 hours.
5. Preheat your oven to 450°F (230°C).
6. Remove the duck legs from the bags and place them on a baking sheet lined with parchment paper.
7. Roast the duck legs in the oven for 15-20 minutes until the skin is crispy.
8. Serve with a side of mashed potatoes or roasted vegetables.

Nutrition: Calories: 400kcal; Fat: 30g; Carb: 1g; Protein: 25g

74. Bison Steak

Preparation Time: 10 minutes

Cooking Time: 3 hours

Servings: 2

Ingredients:

- 2 bison steaks
- 2 tablespoons olive oil
- 1 tablespoon fresh thyme leaves
- 1 tablespoon fresh rosemary, chopped
- Salt and pepper to taste

Directions:

1. Preheat the sous vide water bath to 130°F (54°C).Season the bison steaks with salt, pepper, fresh thyme leaves, and chopped rosemary. Drizzle with olive oil.
2. Place the seasoned steaks in a vacuum-sealed bag and seal.
3. Cook the bison steaks in the water bath for 3 hours.
4. Remove the steaks from the bag and pat dry with paper towels.
5. Sear the steaks on a hot grill or pan for 1-2 minutes per side.
6. Serve with a side salad or roasted vegetables.

Nutrition: Calories: 350kcal; Fat: 20g; Carb: 0g; Protein: 40g

75. Whole Chicken

Preparation Time: 20 minutes

Cooking Time: 4 hours

Servings: 4

Ingredients:

- 1 whole chicken (about 4 lbs)
- 2 tablespoons olive oil
- 2 garlic cloves, minced
- 1 tablespoon fresh thyme leaves
- 1 tablespoon fresh rosemary, chopped
- Salt and pepper to taste

Directions:

1. Preheat the sous vide water bath to 150°F (66°C).
2. Rinse the chicken under cold water and pat dry with paper towels.
3. Season the chicken with salt, pepper, minced garlic, fresh thyme, and chopped rosemary. Drizzle with olive oil.
4. Place the seasoned chicken in a large vacuum-sealed bag and seal.
5. Cook the chicken in the water bath for 4 hours.
6. Preheat your oven to 425°F (220°C).
7. Remove the chicken from the bag and place it on a roasting pan.
8. Roast the chicken in the oven for 30-40 minutes until the skin is crispy and golden brown.
9. Let the chicken rest for a few minutes before carving and serving.

Nutrition: Calories: 300kcal; Fat: 15g; Carb: 0g; Protein: 35g

Chapter 8.   Vegetables

76. Asparagus

Preparation Time: 10 minutes

Cooking Time: 30 minutes

Servings: 4

Ingredients:

- 1 bunch of asparagus
- 2 tablespoons olive oil
- 2 cloves garlic, minced
- Salt and pepper to taste

Directions:

1. Trim the tough ends of the asparagus and place them in a vacuum-sealed bag with olive oil, garlic, salt, and pepper.
2. Seal the bag using a vacuum sealer and cook in the sous vide water bath at 180°F (82°C) for 30 minutes.
3. Once done, remove from the bag and serve hot.

Nutrition: Calories: 80kcal; Fat: 7g; Carb: 4g; Protein: 2g

77. Carrots

Preparation Time: 15 minutes

Cooking Time: 1 hour

Servings: 6

Ingredients:

- 1 pound baby carrots
- 2 tablespoons butter
- 1 tablespoon honey
- 1 teaspoon fresh thyme leaves
- Salt and pepper to taste

Directions:

1. Place the baby carrots in a vacuum-sealed bag with butter, honey, thyme, salt, and pepper.
2. Seal the bag using a vacuum sealer and cook in the sous vide water bath at 185°F (85°C) for 1 hour.
3. Remove from the bag and serve warm.

Nutrition: Calories: 110kcal; Fat: 5g; Carb: 16g; Protein: 1g

78. Sous Vide Broccoli

Preparation Time: 10 minutes

Cooking Time: 45 minutes

Servings: 4

Ingredients:

- 1 head of broccoli, cut into florets
- 2 tablespoons olive oil
- 1 teaspoon lemon zest
- 1 teaspoon garlic powder
- Salt and pepper to taste

Directions:

1. Place the broccoli florets in a vacuum-sealed bag with olive oil, lemon zest, garlic powder, salt, and pepper.
2. Seal the bag using a vacuum sealer and cook in the sous vide water bath at 185°F (85°C) for 45 minutes.
3. Remove from the bag and serve with a squeeze of lemon juice if desired.

Nutrition: Calories: 80kcal; Fat: 6g; Carb: 6g; Protein: 3g

79. Cauliflower Steaks

Preparation Time: 15 minutes

Cooking Time: 1 hour and 15 minutes

Servings: 4

Ingredients:

- 1 large head of cauliflower, sliced into steaks
- 2 tablespoons olive oil
- 1 tablespoon smoked paprika
- 1 teaspoon garlic powder
- Salt and pepper to taste

Directions:

1. Place the cauliflower steaks in a vacuum-sealed bag with olive oil, smoked paprika, garlic powder, salt, and pepper.
2. Seal the bag using a vacuum sealer and cook in the sous vide water bath at 185°F (85°C) for 1 hour and 15 minutes.
3. Finish by searing the cauliflower steaks on a hot grill or in a skillet for a few minutes on each side until golden brown.

Nutrition: Calories: 120kcal; Fat: 7g; Carb: 11g; Protein: 5g

80. Beets

Preparation Time: 10 minutes

Cooking Time: 2 hours

Servings: 4

Ingredients:

- 4 medium-sized beets, peeled and quartered
- 2 tablespoons balsamic vinegar
- 1 tablespoon olive oil
- 1 teaspoon dried thyme
- Salt and pepper to taste

Directions:

1. Place the beets in a vacuum-sealed bag with balsamic vinegar, olive oil, dried thyme, salt, and pepper.
2. Seal the bag using a vacuum sealer and cook in the sous vide water bath at 185°F (85°C) for 2 hours.
3. Once done, remove from the bag and serve as a side dish or in salads.

Nutrition: Calories: 100kcal; Fat: 4g; Carb: 16g; Protein: 2g

81. Green Beans

Preparation Time: 10 minutes

Cooking Time: 40 minutes

Servings: 4

Ingredients:

- 1 pound green beans, trimmed
- 2 tablespoons butter
- 1 tablespoon lemon juice
- 1 teaspoon lemon zest
- Salt and pepper to taste

Directions:

1. Place the green beans in a vacuum-sealed bag with butter, lemon juice, lemon zest, salt, and pepper.
2. Seal the bag using a vacuum sealer and cook in the sous vide water bath at 185°F (85°C) for 40 minutes.
3. Remove from the bag and serve hot.

Nutrition: Calories: 80kcal; Fat: 3g; Carb: 8g; Protein: 2g

82. Brussels Sprout

Preparation Time: 15 minutes

Cooking Time: 1 hour

Servings: 4

Ingredients:

- 1 pound Brussels sprouts, halved
- 2 tablespoons olive oil
- 1 tablespoon balsamic vinegar
- 1 teaspoon dried thyme
- Salt and pepper to taste

Directions:

1. Place the halved Brussels sprouts in a vacuum-sealed bag with olive oil, balsamic vinegar, dried thyme, salt, and pepper.
2. Seal the bag using a vacuum sealer and cook in the sous vide water bath at 185°F (85°C) for 1 hour.
3. Finish by roasting the Brussels sprouts in the oven at 425°F (220°C) for 10 minutes for extra crispiness.

Nutrition: Calories: 100kcal; Fat: 6g; Carb: 10g; Protein: 4g

83. Eggplant

Preparation Time: 20 minutes

Cooking Time: 1 hour and 30 minutes

Servings: 4

Ingredients:

- 1 large eggplant, sliced into rounds
- 2 tablespoons olive oil
- 2 teaspoons dried oregano
- 1 teaspoon garlic powder
- Salt and pepper to taste

Directions:

1. Place the eggplant rounds in a vacuum-sealed bag with olive oil, dried oregano, garlic powder, salt, and pepper.
2. Seal the bag using a vacuum sealer and cook in the sous vide water bath at 185°F (85°C) for 1 hour and 30 minutes.
3. Once done, remove from the bag and serve as a side dish or in sandwiches.

Nutrition: Calories: 90kcal; Fat: 6g; Carb: 9g; Protein: 2g

84. Sweet Potatoes

Preparation Time: 10 minutes

Cooking Time: 1 hour and 15 minutes

Servings: 4

Ingredients:

- 2 large sweet potatoes, peeled and cut into chunks
- 2 tablespoons butter
- 1 tablespoon maple syrup
- 1 teaspoon ground cinnamon
- Salt to taste

Directions:

1. Place the sweet potato chunks in a vacuum-sealed bag with butter, maple syrup, ground cinnamon, and salt.
2. Seal the bag using a vacuum sealer and cook in the sous vide water bath at 185°F (85°C) for 1 hour and 15 minutes.
3. Remove from the bag and serve hot.

Nutrition: Calories: 150kcal; Fat: 5g; Carb: 25g; Protein: 2g

85. Zucchini

Preparation Time: 10 minutes

Cooking Time: 40 minutes

Servings: 4

Ingredients:

- 2 medium zucchinis, sliced
- 2 tablespoons olive oil
- 1 teaspoon dried basil
- 1 teaspoon dried oregano
- Salt and pepper to taste

Directions:

1. Place the zucchini slices in a vacuum-sealed bag with olive oil, dried basil, dried oregano, salt, and pepper.
2. Seal the bag using a vacuum sealer and cook in the sous vide water bath at 185°F (85°C) for 40 minutes.
3. Finish by searing the zucchini slices on a hot grill or in a skillet for a few minutes on each side until tender and slightly charred.

Nutrition: Calories: 80kcal; Fat: 6g; Carb: 5g; Protein: 2g

86. Bell Peppers

Preparation Time: 15 minutes

Cooking Time: 1 hour

Servings: 4

Ingredients:

- 2 bell peppers (any color), sliced
- 2 tablespoons olive oil
- 1 teaspoon dried thyme
- 1 teaspoon paprika
- Salt and pepper to taste

Directions:

1. Place the bell pepper slices in a vacuum-sealed bag with olive oil, dried thyme, paprika, salt, and pepper.
2. Seal the bag using a vacuum sealer and cook in the sous vide water bath at 185°F (85°C) for 1 hour.
3. Remove from the bag and serve as a side dish or use them in sandwiches, salads, or wraps.

Nutrition: Calories: 70kcal; Fat: 5g; Carb: 6g; Protein: 1g

87. Corn on the Cob

Preparation Time: 5 minutes

Cooking Time: 1 hour

Servings: 4

Ingredients:

- 4 ears of corn, husks removed
- 2 tablespoons butter
- 1 teaspoon chili powder
- Salt and pepper to taste

Directions:

1. Place the corn on the cob in a vacuum-sealed bag with butter, chili powder, salt, and pepper.
2. Seal the bag using a vacuum sealer and cook in the sous vide water bath at 183°F (84°C) for 1 hour.
3. Finish by grilling the corn on the cob for a few minutes on each side for a smoky flavor.

Nutrition: Calories: 150kcal; Fat: 6g; Carb: 23g; Protein: 3g

88. Mushrooms

Preparation Time: 10 minutes

Cooking Time: 1 hour

Servings: 4

Ingredients:

- 1 pound mixed mushrooms (cremini, shiitake, oyster, etc.)
- 2 tablespoons butter
- 2 cloves garlic, minced
- 1 teaspoon fresh thyme leaves

- Salt and pepper to taste

Directions:

1. Clean and trim the mushrooms as needed, then place them in a vacuum-sealed bag with butter, minced garlic, fresh thyme, salt, and pepper.

2. Seal the bag using a vacuum sealer and cook in the sous vide water bath at 185°F (85°C) for 1 hour.

3. Remove from the bag and serve as a side dish or use them in omelets, pasta, or risotto.

Nutrition: Calories: 90kcal; Fat: 6g; Carb: 7g; Protein: 4g

89. Cherry Tomatoes

Preparation Time: 5 minutes

Cooking Time: 30 minutes

Servings: 4

Ingredients:

- 1 pint cherry tomatoes
- 2 tablespoons olive oil
- 1 teaspoon dried basil
- Salt and pepper to taste

Directions:

1. Place the cherry tomatoes in a vacuum-sealed bag with olive oil, dried basil, salt, and pepper.

2. Seal the bag using a vacuum sealer and cook in the sous vide water bath at 183°F (84°C) for 30 minutes.

3. Serve as a flavorful topping for salads, pasta, or as a side dish.

Nutrition: Calories: 60kcal; Fat: 4g; Carb: 5g; Protein: 1g

90. Butternut Squash

Preparation Time: 15 minutes

Cooking Time: 1 hour and 30 minutes

Servings: 4

Ingredients:

- 1 medium butternut squash, peeled and cut into cubes
- 2 tablespoons olive oil
- 1 tablespoon maple syrup
- 1 teaspoon ground cinnamon
- Salt to taste

Directions:

1. Place the butternut squash cubes in a vacuum-sealed bag with olive oil, maple syrup, ground cinnamon, and salt.

2. Seal the bag using a vacuum sealer and cook in the sous vide water bath at 185°F (85°C) for 1 hour and 30 minutes.
3. Remove from the bag and serve hot.

Nutrition: Calories: 120kcal; Fat: 6g; Carb: 18g; Protein: 1g

Chapter 9. Sides

91. Garlic Butter Asparagus

Preparation Time: 10 minutes

Cooking Time: 30 minutes

Servings: 4

Ingredients:

- 1 bunch of asparagus, trimmed
- 2 tablespoons unsalted butter, melted
- 2 cloves garlic, minced
- Salt and pepper to taste

Directions:

Preheat the sous vide water bath to 180°F (82°C).

In a bowl, mix melted butter, minced garlic, salt, and pepper.

Divide the asparagus into bundles and wrap each bundle with aluminum foil.

Pour the garlic butter mixture over the asparagus bundles and seal them tightly.

Place the foil-wrapped bundles in a sous vide bag and seal.

Cook in the water bath for 30 minutes.

Remove from the water bath, open the foil packets, and serve immediately.

Nutrition: Calories: 90kcal; Fat: 7g; Carb: 6g; Protein: 3g

92. Lemon Dill Carrots

Preparation Time: 10 minutes

Cooking Time: 1 hour

Servings: 6

Ingredients:

- 1 pound baby carrots
- 2 tablespoons olive oil
- 2 tablespoons fresh dill, chopped
- Zest of 1 lemon
- Juice of half a lemon
- Salt and pepper to taste

Directions:

Preheat the sous vide water bath to 185°F (85°C).

In a bowl, toss the baby carrots with olive oil, chopped dill, lemon zest, lemon juice, salt, and pepper.

Place the seasoned carrots in a sous vide bag and seal.

Cook in the water bath for 1 hour.

Remove from the water bath and serve immediately.

Nutrition: Calories: 80kcal; Fat: 5g; Carb: 8g; Protein: 1g

93. Balsamic Glazed Brussels Sprouts

Preparation Time: 15 minutes

Cooking Time: 1 hour

Servings: 4

Ingredients:

- 1 pound Brussels sprouts, trimmed and halved
- 2 tablespoons olive oil
- 2 tablespoons balsamic vinegar
- 1 tablespoon honey
- Salt and pepper to taste

Directions:

Preheat the sous vide water bath to 185°F (85°C).

In a bowl, toss the Brussels sprouts with olive oil, balsamic vinegar, honey, salt, and pepper.

Place the seasoned Brussels sprouts in a sous vide bag and seal.

Cook in the water bath for 1 hour.

Remove from the water bath, and sear the Brussels sprouts in a hot skillet for 2 minutes on each side for added texture (optional).

Serve immediately.

Nutrition: Calories: 120kcal; Fat: 7g; Carb: 13g; Protein: 4g

94. Herb-Roasted Potatoes

Preparation Time: 15 minutes

Cooking Time: 1 hour

Servings: 4

Ingredients:

- 1 pound baby potatoes, halved
- 2 tablespoons olive oil
- 1 tablespoon fresh rosemary, chopped
- 1 tablespoon fresh thyme, chopped
- 2 cloves garlic, minced
- Salt and pepper to taste

Directions:

Preheat the sous vide water bath to 185°F (85°C).

In a bowl, toss the halved baby potatoes with olive oil, chopped rosemary, chopped thyme, minced garlic, salt, and pepper.

Place the seasoned potatoes in a sous vide bag and seal.

Cook in the water bath for 1 hour.

Remove from the water bath and transfer the potatoes to a baking sheet.

Broil in the oven for 5 minutes or until the potatoes are crispy on the outside.

Serve immediately.

Nutrition: Calories: 180kcal; Fat: 8g; Carb: 25g; Protein: 3g

95. Sesame Green Beans

Preparation Time: 10 minutes

Cooking Time: 1 hour

Servings: 4

Ingredients:

- 1 pound green beans, trimmed
- 2 tablespoons soy sauce
- 1 tablespoon sesame oil
- 1 tablespoon sesame seeds
- 1 teaspoon garlic powder
- Salt and pepper to taste

Directions:

Preheat the sous vide water bath to 185°F (85°C).

In a bowl, mix soy sauce, sesame oil, sesame seeds, garlic powder, salt, and pepper.

Toss the green beans in the sesame mixture until coated.

Place the seasoned green beans in a sous vide bag and seal.

Cook in the water bath for 1 hour.

Remove from the water bath, and sear the green beans in a hot skillet for 2 minutes for added texture (optional).

Serve immediately.

Nutrition: Calories: 70kcal; Fat: 4g; Carb: 7g; Protein: 2g

96. Brown Sugar Glazed Carrots

Preparation Time: 10 minutes

Cooking Time: 1 hour

Servings: 4

Ingredients:

- 1 pound baby carrots
- 2 tablespoons unsalted butter
- 2 tablespoons brown sugar
- 1 tablespoon maple syrup
- 1/2 teaspoon ground cinnamon
- Salt and pepper to taste

Directions:

Preheat the sous vide water bath to 185°F (85°C).

In a bowl, mix melted butter, brown sugar, maple syrup, ground cinnamon, salt, and pepper.

Toss the baby carrots in the brown sugar mixture until coated.

Place the seasoned carrots in a sous vide bag and seal.

Cook in the water bath for 1 hour.

Remove from the water bath and serve immediately.

Nutrition: Calories: 120kcal; Fat: 5g; Carb: 18g; Protein: 1g

97. Creamy Parmesan Corn

Preparation Time: 10 minutes

Cooking Time: 1 hour

Servings: 4

Ingredients:

- 4 cups fresh or frozen corn kernels
- 1 cup heavy cream
- 1/2 cup grated Parmesan cheese
- 2 tablespoons unsalted butter
- 1 tablespoon chopped fresh parsley
- Salt and pepper to taste

Directions:

Preheat the sous vide water bath to 183°F (84°C).

In a bowl, mix corn kernels, heavy cream, grated Parmesan cheese, chopped parsley, salt, and pepper.

Place the corn mixture in a sous vide bag and seal.

Cook in the water bath for 1 hour.

Remove from the water bath, transfer to a serving dish, and top with additional grated Parmesan and parsley if desired.

Serve immediately.

Nutrition: Calories: 350kcal; Fat: 24g; Carb: 27g; Protein: 8g

98. Lemon Herb Artichokes

Preparation Time: 15 minutes

Cooking Time: 2 hours

Servings: 4

Ingredients:

- 4 large artichokes, trimmed and halved
- 2 tablespoons olive oil
- Zest of 1 lemon
- Juice of 1 lemon
- 2 cloves garlic, minced
- 1 tablespoon chopped fresh parsley
- Salt and pepper to taste

Directions:

Preheat the sous vide water bath to 185°F (85°C).

In a bowl, mix olive oil, lemon zest, lemon juice, minced garlic, chopped parsley, salt, and pepper.

Toss the halved artichokes in the lemon herb mixture until coated.

Place the seasoned artichokes in a sous vide bag and seal.

Cook in the water bath for 2 hours.

Remove from the water bath and serve immediately.

Nutrition: Calories: 180kcal; Fat: 9g; Carb: 22g; Protein: 4g

99. Truffle Butter Mushrooms

Preparation Time: 10 minutes

Cooking Time: 1 hour

Servings: 4

Ingredients:

- 1 pound mixed mushrooms (e.g., cremini, shiitake, oyster), cleaned and sliced
- 2 tablespoons truffle oil
- 2 tablespoons unsalted butter
- 2 cloves garlic, minced
- 1 tablespoon chopped fresh thyme
- Salt and pepper to taste

Directions:

Preheat the sous vide water bath to 185°F (85°C).

In a bowl, mix truffle oil, melted butter, minced garlic, chopped thyme, salt, and pepper.

Toss the sliced mushrooms in the truffle butter mixture until coated.

Place the seasoned mushrooms in a sous vide bag and seal.

Cook in the water bath for 1 hour.

Remove from the water bath and serve immediately.

Nutrition: Calories: 120kcal; Fat: 10g; Carb: 5g; Protein: 3g

100.   Honey Glazed Beets

Preparation Time: 15 minutes

Cooking Time: 2 hours

Servings: 4

Ingredients:

- 1 pound beets, peeled and sliced
- 2 tablespoons honey
- 1 tablespoon balsamic vinegar
- 1 tablespoon olive oil
- Salt and pepper to taste

Directions:

Preheat the sous vide water bath to 183°F (84°C).

In a bowl, mix honey, balsamic vinegar, olive oil, salt, and pepper.

Toss the sliced beets in the honey glaze mixture until coated.

Place the seasoned beets in a sous vide bag and seal.

Cook in the water bath for 2 hours.

Remove from the water bath and serve immediately.

Nutrition: Calories: 120kcal; Fat: 4g; Carb: 20g; Protein: 2g

Chapter 10. Desserts

101. Chocolate Lava Cake

Preparation Time: 15 minutes

Cooking Time: 1 hour

Servings: 4

Ingredients:

- 1/2 cup semi-sweet chocolate chips
- 1/4 cup unsalted butter
- 1/4 cup all-purpose flour
- 1/2 cup powdered sugar
- 2 large eggs
- 1 teaspoon vanilla extract
- Pinch of salt
- Cooking spray

Directions:

1. Preheat the sous vide water bath to 176°F (80°C).
2. In a microwave-safe bowl, melt the chocolate chips and butter together.
3. In a separate bowl, whisk together the flour, powdered sugar, eggs, vanilla extract, and salt until well combined.
4. Slowly pour the melted chocolate mixture into the egg mixture while whisking continuously.
5. Lightly grease four 4-ounce ramekins with cooking spray and pour the batter evenly into each.
6. Seal the ramekins with plastic wrap or lids and place them in the sous vide water bath.
7. Cook for 1 hour.
8. Remove the ramekins from the water bath, carefully uncover them, and serve the lava cakes warm with a dusting of powdered sugar.

Nutrition: Calories: 300kcal; Fat: 18g; Carb: 32g; Protein: 5g

102. Creme Brulee

Preparation Time: 10 minutes

Cooking Time: 1 hour 30 minutes

Servings: 6

Ingredients:

- 2 cups heavy cream

- 1/2 cup granulated sugar
- 1 teaspoon vanilla extract
- 6 large egg yolks
- 6 teaspoons granulated sugar (for caramelizing)

Directions:

1. Preheat the sous vide water bath to 176°F (80°C).
2. In a saucepan, heat the heavy cream and 1/2 cup granulated sugar over medium heat, stirring until the sugar dissolves. Remove from heat, add vanilla extract, and let it cool slightly.
3. In a separate bowl, whisk the egg yolks until smooth.
4. Slowly pour the cream mixture into the egg yolks while whisking continuously to create the custard.
5. Strain the custard through a fine mesh sieve into a large measuring cup.
6. Divide the custard among six 4-ounce ramekins.
7. Seal the ramekins with plastic wrap or lids and place them in the sous vide water bath.
8. Cook for 1 hour and 30 minutes.
9. Remove the ramekins from the water bath, let them cool, and refrigerate for at least 2 hours.
10. Sprinkle 1 teaspoon of granulated sugar on each custard and caramelize using a kitchen torch before serving.

Nutrition: Calories: 400kcal; Fat: 34g; Carb: 21g; Protein: 6g

103.   Lemon Cheesecake

Preparation Time: 20 minutes

Cooking Time: 1 hour 30 minutes

Servings: 8

Ingredients:

- 1 1/2 cups graham cracker crumbs
- 1/4 cup granulated sugar
- 1/2 cup unsalted butter, melted
- 16 ounces cream cheese, softened
- 1 cup granulated sugar
- 3 large eggs
- Zest and juice of 1 lemon
- 1 teaspoon vanilla extract

Directions:

1. Preheat the sous vide water bath to 176°F (80°C).
2. In a bowl, mix graham cracker crumbs, 1/4 cup granulated sugar, and melted butter until well combined.
3. Press the mixture into the bottom of a 9-inch springform pan to form the crust.

4. In a separate bowl, beat the softened cream cheese and 1 cup granulated sugar until smooth.

5. Add the eggs, lemon zest, lemon juice, and vanilla extract to the cream cheese mixture and mix until fully combined.

6. Pour the cheesecake batter over the crust in the springform pan.

7. Cover the pan tightly with aluminum foil and place it in the sous vide water bath.

8. Cook for 1 hour and 30 minutes.

9. Remove the cheesecake from the water bath, let it cool, and refrigerate for at least 4 hours before serving.

Nutrition: Calories: 500kcal; Fat: 38g; Carb: 35g; Protein: 8g

104. Vanilla Poached Pears

Preparation Time: 15 minutes

Cooking Time: 1 hour 30 minutes

Servings: 4

Ingredients:

- 4 ripe but firm pears, peeled and cored
- 2 cups water
- 1/2 cup granulated sugar
- 1 vanilla bean, split and seeds scraped
- Zest of 1 orange
- 1 cinnamon stick

Directions:

1. Preheat the sous vide water bath to 176°F (80°C).

2. In a saucepan, combine water, granulated sugar, vanilla bean and seeds, orange zest, and cinnamon stick. Bring to a simmer, stirring until the sugar dissolves.

3. Add the peeled and cored pears to the simmering liquid and cook for 5 minutes.

4. Remove the pears from the liquid and place them in a sous vide bag or a vacuum-sealed bag.

5. Pour the simmering liquid over the pears in the bag, and seal the bag tightly.

6. Place the bag in the sous vide water bath and cook for 1 hour and 30 minutes.

7. Remove the pears from the water bath, let them cool, and serve with a drizzle of the poaching liquid.

Nutrition: Calories: 180kcal; Fat: 0.5g; Carb: 44g; Protein: 1g

105. Coconut Flan

Preparation Time: 15 minutes

Cooking Time: 1 hour 30 minutes

Servings: 6

Ingredients:

- 1 cup coconut milk
- 1 cup whole milk
- 1/2 cup sweetened condensed milk
- 4 large eggs
- 1 teaspoon vanilla extract
- 1/4 cup granulated sugar (for caramelizing)

Directions:

1. Preheat the sous vide water bath to 176°F (80°C).
2. In a saucepan, heat the coconut milk, whole milk, and sweetened condensed milk over medium heat until warm (do not boil).
3. In a separate bowl, whisk the eggs and vanilla extract until well combined.
4. Slowly pour the warm milk mixture into the egg mixture while whisking continuously to create the flan custard.
5. Strain the custard through a fine mesh sieve into a large measuring cup.
6. In a small saucepan, melt the granulated sugar over medium heat until it turns into a caramel.
7. Divide the caramel evenly among six 4-ounce ramekins.
8. Pour the flan custard over the caramel in each ramekin.
9. Seal the ramekins with plastic wrap or lids and place them in the sous vide water bath.
10. Cook for 1 hour and 30 minutes.
11. Remove the ramekins from the water bath, let them cool, and refrigerate for at least 4 hours before serving. Invert the flans onto serving plates before serving.

Nutrition: Calories: 250kcal; Fat: 14g; Carb: 25g; Protein: 8g

106.   Poached Apricots with Honey and Thyme

Preparation Time: 10 minutes

Cooking Time: 1 hour

Servings: 4

Ingredients:

- 8 fresh apricots, halved and pitted
- 1/2 cup honey
- Zest and juice of 1 lemon
- 4 sprigs fresh thyme

Directions:

1. Preheat the sous vide water bath to 176°F (80°C).
2. In a bowl, mix honey, lemon zest, and lemon juice until well combined.
3. Toss the halved and pitted apricots in the honey mixture until they are coated.
4. Place the apricots and fresh thyme sprigs in a sous vide bag or a vacuum-sealed bag.

5. Seal the bag tightly.
6. Place the bag in the sous vide water bath and cook for 1 hour.
7. Remove the bag from the water bath, let the apricots cool slightly, and serve with a drizzle of the honey mixture.

Nutrition: Calories: 140kcal; Fat: 0g; Carb: 36g; Protein: 1g

107. Raspberry Cheesecake Jars

Preparation Time: 20 minutes

Cooking Time: 1 hour 30 minutes

Servings: 4

Ingredients:

- 1 cup graham cracker crumbs
- 2 tablespoons granulated sugar
- 1/4 cup unsalted butter, melted
- 8 ounces cream cheese, softened
- 1/2 cup granulated sugar
- 1/2 cup sour cream
- 1 teaspoon vanilla extract
- 1 cup fresh raspberries

Directions:

1. Preheat the sous vide water bath to 176°F (80°C).
2. In a bowl, mix graham cracker crumbs, 2 tablespoons granulated sugar, and melted butter until well combined.
3. Divide the mixture among four 8-ounce mason jars and press it down to form the crust.
4. In a separate bowl, beat the softened cream cheese, 1/2 cup granulated sugar, sour cream, and vanilla extract until smooth.
5. Gently fold in the fresh raspberries into the cream cheese mixture.
6. Divide the cream cheese mixture evenly among the mason jars over the crust.
7. Seal the jars with lids or use sous vide jar attachment and place them in the sous vide water bath.
8. Cook for 1 hour and 30 minutes.
9. Remove the jars from the water bath, let them cool, and refrigerate for at least 2 hours before serving.

Nutrition: Calories: 550kcal; Fat: 37g; Carb: 50g; Protein: 8g

108. Banana Bread Pudding

Preparation Time: 20 minutes

Cooking Time: 2 hours

Servings: 6

Ingredients:

- 4 cups day-old bread cubes (such as brioche or challah)
- 2 ripe bananas, mashed
- 2 cups whole milk
- 1/2 cup granulated sugar
- 3 large eggs
- 1 teaspoon vanilla extract
- 1/2 teaspoon ground cinnamon
- Pinch of salt

Directions:

1. Preheat the sous vide water bath to 176°F (80°C).
2. In a large bowl, mix mashed bananas, whole milk, granulated sugar, eggs, vanilla extract, ground cinnamon, and salt until well combined.
3. Gently fold in the day-old bread cubes into the banana mixture.
4. Divide the bread pudding mixture among six 4-ounce ramekins.
5. Seal the ramekins with plastic wrap or lids and place them in the sous vide water bath.
6. Cook for 2 hours.
7. Remove the ramekins from the water bath, let them cool slightly, and serve warm.

Nutrition: Calories: 320kcal; Fat: 8g; Carb: 54g; Protein: 9g

109. Poached Apples with Caramel Sauce

Preparation Time: 15 minutes

Cooking Time: 1 hour

Servings: 4

Ingredients:

- 4 apples, peeled, cored, and halved
- 2 cups apple cider
- 1/4 cup granulated sugar
- 1 teaspoon ground cinnamon
- 1/4 cup heavy cream
- 1/4 cup brown sugar
- 1/4 cup unsalted butter
- Pinch of salt

Directions:

1. Preheat the sous vide water bath to 176°F (80°C).
2. In a saucepan, heat the apple cider, granulated sugar, and ground cinnamon over medium heat, stirring until the sugar dissolves.

3. Add the peeled, cored, and halved apples to the simmering liquid and cook for 5 minutes.

4. Remove the apples from the liquid and place them in a sous vide bag or a vacuum-sealed bag.

5. Pour the simmering liquid over the apples in the bag, and seal the bag tightly.

6. Place the bag in the sous vide water bath and cook for 1 hour.

7. In a separate saucepan, melt the brown sugar and unsalted butter over medium heat until it forms a caramel.

8. Stir in the heavy cream and a pinch of salt until the caramel sauce is smooth.

9. Remove the apples from the bag, let them cool slightly, and serve with a drizzle of the caramel sauce.

Nutrition: Calories: 350kcal; Fat: 14g; Carb: 59g; Protein: 2g

110. Maple Pecan Bread Pudding

Preparation Time: 20 minutes

Cooking Time: 2 hours

Servings: 6

Ingredients:

- 4 cups day-old bread cubes (such as French bread)
- 1 cup whole milk
- 1 cup heavy cream
- 1/2 cup pure maple syrup
- 3 large eggs
- 1 teaspoon vanilla extract
- 1/2 cup chopped pecans
- Pinch of salt

Directions:

1. Preheat the sous vide water bath to 176°F (80°C).

2. In a large bowl, whisk together the whole milk, heavy cream, pure maple syrup, eggs, vanilla extract, and a pinch of salt until well combined.

3. Gently fold in the day-old bread cubes and chopped pecans into the maple mixture.

4. Divide the bread pudding mixture among six 4-ounce ramekins.

5. Seal the ramekins with plastic wrap or lids and place them in the sous vide water bath.

6. Cook for 2 hours.

7. Remove the ramekins from the water bath, let them cool slightly, and serve warm.

Nutrition: Calories: 550kcal; Fat: 34g; Carb: 50g; Protein: 9g

Chapter 11. Beverages

111.　Mulled Wine

Preparation Time: 10 minutes

Cooking Time: 2 hours

Servings: 4

Ingredients:

- `1 bottle red wine
- 1/4 cup honey
- 1 orange, sliced
- 1 cinnamon stick
- 4 whole cloves
- 2 star anise
- 1/2 cup brandy (optional)

Directions:

1. In a large sealable bag, combine the red wine, honey, orange slices, cinnamon stick, cloves, and star anise. Add brandy if desired for a stronger kick.
2. Seal the bag using the water displacement method and place it in a preheated water bath set to 140°F (60°C).
3. Sous vide the mixture for 2 hours to infuse the flavors.
4. Remove the bag from the water bath, strain the mulled wine into mugs, and serve warm.

Nutrition: Calories: 200kcal; Fat: 0g; Carb: 25g; Protein: 1g

112.　Lemon Ginger Tea

Preparation Time: 5 minutes

Cooking Time: 1 hour

Servings: 2

Ingredients:

- 2 cups water
- 2 tablespoons honey
- 1 lemon, thinly sliced
- 2-inch piece fresh ginger, peeled and sliced

Directions:

1. In a sealable bag, combine water, honey, lemon slices, and ginger.
2. Seal the bag and place it in a preheated water bath set to 160°F (71°C).

3. Sous vide the mixture for 1 hour to infuse the flavors.

4. Strain the tea into cups and serve hot.

Nutrition: Calories: 60kcal; Fat: 0g; Carb: 17g; Protein: 0g

113.   Iced Coffee

Preparation Time: 5 minutes

Cooking Time: 2 hours

Servings: 4

Ingredients:

- 4 cups water
- 1/2 cup coarsely ground coffee beans
- 1/4 cup condensed milk
- Ice cubes

Directions:

1. In a large sealable bag, combine water and coffee grounds.

2. Seal the bag using the water displacement method and place it in a preheated water bath set to 165°F (74°C).

3. Sous vide the coffee mixture for 2 hours to extract the flavors.

4. Remove the bag from the water bath and strain the coffee into a pitcher.

5. Stir in condensed milk until well combined.

6. Serve the iced coffee over ice cubes.

Nutrition: Calories: 80kcal; Fat: 2g; Carb: 14g; Protein: 2g

114.   Spiced Hot Chocolate

Preparation Time: 5 minutes

Cooking Time: 1 hour

Servings: 2

Ingredients:

- 2 cups milk
- 1/4 cup unsweetened cocoa powder
- 2 tablespoons sugar
- 1/2 teaspoon ground cinnamon
- 1/4 teaspoon ground nutmeg
- 1/4 teaspoon vanilla extract
- Pinch of salt
- Whipped cream and chocolate shavings for garnish

Directions:

1. In a sealable bag, combine milk, cocoa powder, sugar, cinnamon, nutmeg, vanilla extract, and salt.
2. Seal the bag and place it in a preheated water bath set to 165°F (74°C).
3. Sous vide the hot chocolate mixture for 1 hour to infuse the flavors.
4. Remove the bag from the water bath and pour the hot chocolate into mugs.
5. Top with whipped cream and chocolate shavings before serving.

Nutrition: Calories: 180kcal; Fat: 5g; Carb: 32g; Protein: 8g

115.   Chai Latte

Preparation Time: 10 minutes

Cooking Time: 2 hours

Servings: 4

Ingredients:

- 2 cups whole milk
- 4 chai tea bags
- 2 tablespoons honey
- 1 teaspoon vanilla extract

Directions:

1. In a sealable bag, combine whole milk, chai tea bags, honey, and vanilla extract.
2. Seal the bag using the water displacement method and place it in a preheated water bath set to 155°F (68°C).
3. Sous vide the chai latte mixture for 2 hours to steep the tea.
4. Remove the bag from the water bath, discard the tea bags, and pour the chai latte into cups.
5. Optionally, sprinkle some ground cinnamon on top before serving.

Nutrition: Calories: 120kcal; Fat: 5g; Carb: 15g; Protein: 5g

116.   Raspberry Lemonade

Preparation Time: 5 minutes

Cooking Time: 1 hour

Servings: 2

Ingredients:

- 2 cups water
- 1/2 cup fresh raspberries
- 1/4 cup lemon juice
- 2 tablespoons honey

Directions:

1. In a sealable bag, combine water, fresh raspberries, lemon juice, and honey.
2. Seal the bag and place it in a preheated water bath set to 140°F (60°C).

3. Sous vide the raspberry lemonade mixture for 1 hour to infuse the flavors.

4. Strain the lemonade into glasses and serve over ice.

Nutrition: Calories: 60kcal; Fat: 0g; Carb: 17g; Protein: 1g

117.   Infused Water

Preparation Time: 5 minutes

Cooking Time: 1 hour

Servings: 4

Ingredients:

- 4 cups water
- Sliced fruits (e.g., lemon, lime, cucumber, berries)
- Fresh herbs (e.g., mint, basil)

Directions:

1. In a large sealable bag, combine water and sliced fruits with fresh herbs.

2. Seal the bag using the water displacement method and place it in a preheated water bath set to 130°F (54°C).

3. Sous vide the infused water for 1 hour to release the flavors.

4. Remove the bag from the water bath, strain the infused water into a pitcher, and refrigerate until ready to serve.

Nutrition: Calories: 0kcal; Fat: 0g; Carb: 0g; Protein: 0g

118.   Peppermint Hot Cocoa

Preparation Time: 5 minutes

Cooking Time: 1 hour

Servings: 2

Ingredients:

- 2 cups milk
- 2 tablespoons unsweetened cocoa powder
- 2 tablespoons sugar
- 1/2 teaspoon peppermint extract
- Whipped cream and crushed candy canes for garnish

Directions:

1. In a sealable bag, combine milk, cocoa powder, sugar, and peppermint extract.

2. Seal the bag and place it in a preheated water bath set to 165°F (74°C).

3. Sous vide the hot cocoa mixture for 1 hour to infuse the flavors.

4. Remove the bag from the water bath and pour the hot cocoa into mugs.

5. Top with whipped cream and crushed candy canes before serving.

Nutrition: Calories: 180kcal; Fat: 5g; Carb: 32g; Protein: 8g

119. Cold Brew Coffee

Preparation Time: 5 minutes

Cooking Time: 8 hours (cold brew steeping)

Servings: 4

Ingredients:

- 4 cups cold water
- 1 cup coarsely ground coffee beans
- Milk or cream (optional)
- Sweetener (optional)

Directions:

1. In a large sealable bag, combine cold water and coarsely ground coffee beans.
2. Seal the bag using the water displacement method and refrigerate for 8 hours to cold brew the coffee.
3. After 8 hours, remove the bag from the refrigerator and strain the cold brew coffee through a fine mesh strainer or coffee filter into a pitcher.
4. Serve the cold brew coffee over ice, and optionally add milk or cream and sweetener to taste.

Nutrition: Calories: 0kcal; Fat: 0g; Carb: 0g; Protein: 0g

120. Matcha Latte

Preparation Time: 5 minutes

Cooking Time: 30 minutes

Servings: 2

Ingredients:

- 2 cups milk
- 2 tablespoons matcha powder
- 2 tablespoons honey or sweetener of choice
- 1 teaspoon vanilla extract

Directions:

1. In a sealable bag, combine milk, matcha powder, honey, and vanilla extract.
2. Seal the bag and place it in a preheated water bath set to 155°F (68°C).
3. Sous vide the matcha latte mixture for 30 minutes to blend the flavors and dissolve the matcha powder.
4. Remove the bag from the water bath and whisk the matcha latte until frothy.
5. Pour the matcha latte into cups and enjoy.

Nutrition: Calories: 160kcal; Fat: 5g; Carb: 25g; Protein: 5g

Conclusion

As we come to the end of this Cookbook, we are filled with a sense of wonder at the culinary possibilities that this revolutionary cooking method offers. Throughout the pages of this book, we have explored the ins and outs of sous vide cooking, unlocking its secrets and discovering the incredible potential it holds for home cooks and professional chefs alike. Now, as we conclude this culinary journey, let us reflect on the key takeaways and the impact sous vide has on the world of gastronomy.

Precision and Consistency: One of the primary virtues of sous vide cooking is its unparalleled precision and consistency. By cooking food in a precisely controlled water bath at a specific temperature, you can achieve results that are consistently perfect each time you cook. This method ensures that your steaks are cooked to the exact level of doneness you desire, your vegetables are tender yet vibrant, and your desserts are perfectly set – all without any guesswork.

Enhancing Flavors and Nutrients: Sous vide cooking also shines when it comes to enhancing flavors and preserving nutrients. As food is vacuum-sealed before cooking, it retains its natural juices and flavors, leading to unparalleled taste and tenderness. Additionally, the sealed environment helps to lock in essential vitamins and nutrients that might be lost in traditional cooking methods.

Efficiency and Convenience: Sous vide cooking is remarkably efficient and convenient. With minimal hands-on time, you can prepare large batches of food in advance, saving you precious time during busy weekdays or when entertaining guests. This convenience extends to its ability to reheat or finish dishes, allowing you to enjoy delicious, restaurant-quality meals on-demand.

Versatility in Ingredients: One of the most exciting aspects of sous vide cooking is its versatility with a wide array of ingredients. From meat and fish to vegetables, eggs, and even desserts, this method allows you to explore a diverse range of culinary creations. By experimenting with different ingredients, seasonings, and cooking times, you can unleash your creativity in the kitchen like never before.

Empowerment in the Kitchen: As you've learned throughout this cookbook, sous vide cooking empowers you to take control of your culinary destiny. By understanding the principles and techniques behind this method, you can experiment, innovate, and customize recipes to suit your personal preferences. It encourages you to break free from traditional cooking norms and create your own signature dishes.

Adventures Beyond the Cookbook: Beyond the recipes and techniques detailed in this book, the world of sous vide is vast and constantly evolving. As technology advances, we can expect even more innovative sous vide equipment and accessories to hit the market, further enhancing the sous vide experience. Additionally, chefs and home cooks around the world are continually pushing the boundaries of sous vide cooking, discovering new and exciting ways to utilize this method in their kitchens.

The Sous Vide Community: Throughout your journey into the world of sous vide, you'll find a vibrant and passionate community of culinary enthusiasts. From online forums to social media groups, sous vide lovers come together to share their experiences, exchange ideas, and inspire one another. Joining this community opens up a world of learning and camaraderie, and you'll find yourself enriched by the shared passion for this remarkable cooking technique.

In conclusion, the Sous Vide Cookbook has been designed to serve as your trusty companion in your culinary adventures. We hope that it has not only equipped you with the necessary knowledge and skills to excel in sous vide cooking but also inspired you to explore the endless possibilities it offers. Remember, the key to mastering sous vide lies in practice, experimentation, and an open mind.

Now, armed with the knowledge and recipes from this book, it's time to step into your kitchen with confidence and embark on your own sous vide journey. Embrace the precision, savor the flavors, and enjoy the joy of creating incredible meals that will delight your taste buds and leave a lasting impression on those you share them with. Happy cooking, and bon appétit!

Made in the USA
Las Vegas, NV
04 November 2023